TAROT

Beginner's Guide to the Ageless Wisdom for Self-Improvement and Master the Art of Tarot Card Reading, Including the Meanings of the Ancient Cards and Divination (2022 for Newbies)

Zelene Harrison

TABLE OF CONTENTS

INTRODUCTION ____ 5

   The Tarot's colour implications ___________________________ 6

CHAPTER 1: ____ 8

ORIGIN OF THE TAROT __________________________________ 8

   Numerous Tarot Packs _________________________________ 14

   Tarot Card Fundamentals _______________________________ 17

   Essential Components of a Tarot Deck_____________________ 18

   The Tarot Cards' Utility ________________________________ 20

   Tarot Deck Maintenance________________________________ 21

   Your Tarot Diary _____________________________________ 23

   Important Concepts to Understand _______________________ 25

CHAPTER 2: ____ 29

GETTING ACQUAINTED WITH YOUR DECK __________________ 29

   Reading for your own benefit____________________________ 30

   Five Fundamental Exercises Using a Tarot Deck _____________ 33

   Tarot Card Reading: A Step-by-Step Guide _________________ 35

CHAPTER 3: ____ 40

BEGINNING THE MINOR ARCANA _____________________________ 40

How to Interpret Suit Card Numbers _____________________ 42

The Court Playing Cards ________________________________ 46

CHAPTER 4: ____ 66

BASIC TAROT INTERPRETATION TIPS ______________________ 66

How to Utilize Clarifying Cards __________________________ 70

CHAPTER 5: ____ 73

TAROT RITUALS ____ 73

CHAPTER 6: ____ 77

ENHANCING AND EXPANDING YOUR TAROT READING PROWESS 77

Male and Female _______________________________________ 78

Tarot and Astrology ____________________________________ 78

Seasons and Suits ______________________________________ 80

Cooking, Crystals, and Creativity ________________________ 82

CHAPTER 7: ____ 84

MEDITATION AND MINDFULNESS WITH TAROT______________ 84

The Magician's Personal Power __________________________ 85

The Star and Healing____________________________________ 86

Equilibrium and Temperance ______________________________________ 87

Meditation on Love and the Lovers Card ______________________ 88

CHAPTER 8: ____ 89

DEVELOP YOUR INTUITION THROUGH TAROT ________________ 89

What Exactly Is Intuition?______________________________________ 90

The Magnificence of Images ___________________________________ 90

Visuals, audibles, and sensations ______________________________ 91

Connecting with your Intuition _________________________________ 94

Recognize Warnings ____ 96

Elimination of Negativity ______________________________________ 98

CHAPTER 9: ____ 100

TIPS TO ENSURE A GOOD READING ___________________________ 100

Perfect Practice ____ 103

CONCLUSION ____ 106

INTRODUCTION

The Tarot is a deck of cards comprised of 78 printed cards and one transparent card. It contains 22 Major Arcana (or image) cards and 56 Minor Arcana cards.

The Major Arcana cards have a numerical value of 0–21. Each card has a title, such as the Blockhead or the World. The Major Arcana cards depict the profound meanings behind everyday occurrences, while the Minor Arcana cards detail everyday events. While the Minor Arcana cards may reveal issues in your romantic relationship, the Major Arcana cards reveal the fundamental exercise that must be learned in that situation.

The Minor Arcana is divided into four suits of fourteen cards each. Each suit contains ten cards numbered 1–10 and four Court cards titled Lord, Sovereign, Knight, and Page.

These suits have different names than when playing a card game, but they all refer to the same thing. They consist of the following suits: • Wands (Clubs) • Cups (Hearts) • Swords (Spades) and Pentacles (Diamonds).

At first glance, the horde cards and their numerous variants may appear perplexing. In any case, this visual language is already familiar to your intuitive brain, and thus you will be recalling the cards rather than learning them.

The Tarot is an image book, and once you are aware of these images, the Tarot becomes a portal to recently concealed information and data. The Tarot is a device that promotes physical, passionate, mental, and profound growth and learning. While the Tarot can be used to forecast the future, it is not limited to that. It can also shed light on the fundamental reasons for a situation and reveal the exercises that can be gained from it. This is the ideal exemplified by the well-known axiom: Those who do not benefit from history are doomed to repeat it.

The Tarot can be used to determine the most appropriate course of action in any given situation, which is why we strive to avoid repeating our exercises. The preceding adage reminds us that we are all repeating exercises and that we, collectively, have the option of progressing to all the more difficult choices.

The Tarot's colour implications

Red: Vitality or excitement in approaching life's difficulties. Cards containing red parcels, such as the Sovereign, demonstrate a physical or viable way of dealing with life.

Orange: An energising or exuberant approach to life. Cards with a high proportion of orange (as the Wands cards do) indicate an ardent or hot-blooded approach to life.

Yellow: A scholarly approach to the current situation. Cards with a lot of yellow (for example, Quality and the Sun) demonstrate mental acuity, as well as a consistent concept and investigation.

Green: The colour green is associated with amiability and balance in the Tarot. Few cards in the Rider-Waite deck contain more than a token amount of green.

Blue: Adapted profound comprehension is symbolised in the Tarot by the use of the colour blue. It demonstrates the mind coupled with a profound perspective that encompasses the larger picture of life.

Purple: Sympathy is symbolised in the Tarot by the use of the colour purple.

Purple cards, such as the Darlings (sympathy for an accomplice) or Equity (empathy for strangers), demonstrate that sympathy begins with those closest to us and can grow to include strangers as we mature.

White: In the Tarot, the colour white symbolises purity of intention. For example, the white blossoms in the Six of Cups (when two individuals share a delicate, private moment) or the white lilies and white tunic in the Performer, where he relies on the pure intentions he had in the Blockhead (represented by the snow-capped mountains) to advance to the next card.

CHAPTER 1:

ORIGIN OF THE TAROT

Leaving the tarot card invariably conjures images of old gypsy people posing in front of their crystal ball in a nebular room brimming with strange artefacts. The term "Tarot" also carries an aura of mystery, as no one knows when or how Tarot works. While scholars are aware that the majority of the tarot card's recorded history originates in Italy.

Tarot may have been derived from ancient Egyptian tablets (because identical silent people exist who communicate only through their presence and image, as Egyptian hieroglyphics and some Tarot symbols), or from Chaldean Hidden Texts.

Many believe that the Tarot was brought into Europe following the cruises by the Knights Templars, while others believe that the

Gypsies enjoyed reading the Tarot during their visits to the continent during the Middle Ages.

Additionally, historians discovered evidence that 78-card Tarot decks were used in Italy and France during the Renaissance to reveal fortunes.

According to researchers, these early tarot decks could be a byproduct of modern playing cards.

Regardless of the various interpretations, one thing is certain: for seven hundred years, tarot card reading saw daylight as one of the most important sources of spiritual knowledge in the western world.

According to some tarot historians, the tarot cards originated as a game called Triumph, which is today's equivalent of "Bridge." The game was called "Tarocchi" (later Tarot), and it quickly spread throughout Europe.

The markings on the cards were quickly recognised by mystic practitioners in France and England and were frequently used as a divination device, eventually becoming a component of occult theory.

However, tarot readings were still quite simple during that time period.

By the eighteenth century, tarot readers were assigning specific meanings to each card, and in 1781, a French freemason published an in-depth analysis of the tarot. The Tarot was believed to have been inspired by Egyptian priests' ancient mysteries and to be connected to the stories of Isis, Osiris, and other Egyptian gods.

In 1791, Jean-Baptiste Alliette published the first Tarot box, and interest in occult research grew rapidly due to its popularity among dull upper-class families.

In 1909, Arthur Waite, a British occultist, and artist Pamela Colman Smith published the world's most famous tarot card set, the Rider-Waite deck.

Today, tarot card reading is extremely popular, and an increasing number of people rely on a tarot reading to guide them through their daily lives. Tarot readings assist seekers in contemplating themselves and others, as well as predicting their future. Additionally, these cards can be used for introspection and meditation. The cards are now available in an almost infinite variety of styles. Any deck that the user is comfortable with can be used.

The 78 Tarot cards are divided into the Major Arcana and Minor Arcana, which translates as "great secrets" and "little secrets," respectively. Once upon a time, the Tarot's origins could be traced all the way back to ancient Egypt, with the cards possibly representing the long-lost Egyptian Dead Book. This is the concept that has largely been uncovered since the book's creation and publication, but the concept's appeal and allure remain, and many occultists retain it.

The first to suggest an alternative source was Le Monde Primitif (1781), an encyclopaedic work on anthropological linguistics, and Antoine Court de Gébelin (c. 1719-1784)—the Book of Thoth, another Egyptian text he claimed was the only writing to survive the burning of his libraries and contained the Egyptian empire's pure and most sacred doctrines. He claimed that these doctrines were spread throughout Europe (though diluted) by Gypsies, whom he assumed were descended from the Egyptians (a claim that has since been refuted). He discovered what he believed to be timeless esoteric wisdom arcane in this 78-page book of bizarre figures.

He also claimed to have discovered hints about the Tarot deck's true origins. By combining the words' tar' (' way' or' path') and' royal' (' king' or' royal'), he implied that it should be dictated by the Royal Path of Human Life. He reasoned that Egypt's wise men were anticipating and analysing the future significance of these holy symbols.

Additionally, he discovered hints to the Egyptian symbols in contemporary tarot cards. In his opinion, the Star card represented Sirius, the Dog-star, which rises with the Nile flood at the start of each new year, and the Lady below represented Isis, Queen of Heaven, who strewn water from her vases (the tears of Isis which each year flooded the Nile). He correctly identified the Devil card as Set, the god of chaos and darkness.

However, numerous scholars disputed De Gébelin's findings. Thoth's now fully translated book contains two charms, one of which ostensibly assists the reader in comprehending the animals' language and the other of which encourages the reader to interpret the gods. The story of Thoth, the god of writing and knowledge, includes the book itself, which was said to have been buried near Coptos at the bottom of the Nile and was sealed inside a serpent-protected shell.

Egyptian Prince Neferkaptah fought the serpents and discovered the book, but the gods as a punishment for Thoth's theft killed his son and wife. The Book was misplaced, and Neferkaptah took his own life.

Generations later, despite opposition from the spirit of Neferkaptah, Setne Khamwas, the story's protagonist, steals the book from Neferkaptah's tomb. Rather than that, Setne is seduced by a beautiful woman into murdering and humiliating his children in front of the pharaoh. He discovered the episode to be Neferkaptah's dream, and fearful of further reward, he returned the book to Neferkaptah's tomb, along with a fascinating parable.

The narrative itself does not provide much support for De Gébelin's interpretation of the symbols.

There are numerous other hypotheses, one of which is that Tarot originated from magical numbered cart decks that existed in ancient India and the Far East and could have been transported to Europe by the Templar Knights during and after their Holy Land cruises. Obviously, this hypothesis, like the others, is pure conjecture.

If these games existed, how are we to know they were responsible for the creation of the Tarot?

The truth is that nobody truly understands how the Tarot box came to be. Its true origins remain shrouded in mystery. Even the etymology of the term is uncertain. While de Gébelin suggested an Egyptian term, other historians believe that the term "Torah" is corrupt and that the Hebrew Law Book is interpreted by some as "wheel" and "rota" as an anagram of the Latin word "rota."

So, what do we know for certain about Tarot's genesis?

Between 1430 and 1450, the first known Tarot cards were created between Milan, Ferrara, and Bologna in Northern Italy, possibly when a famed four-suit player card set was expanded to include additional cards trumps with allegorical diagrams. These modern decks were originally known as cartes da trionfi, or trump cards, while the remaining cards became known as trionfi. The first textual evidence of the carte da trionfi's existence is a written statement in Ferrara's court record, 1442. The earliest surviving Tarot cards are fifteen splinter decks created in the middle of the 15th century for Milan's kings, Visconti-Sforza.

This secondary function of the cards gradually evolved into their primary purpose. Eliphas Levi Zahid (1810-1875), like De

Gébelin, studied for the priesthood but then turned to sorcery, mysticism, and occultism. Convinced that the Tarot's origins predate the 14th century, he observed parallels between the Tarot and the Jewish spiritual method known as Kabbalah.

Levi noted that the 22 trumps in the Tarot correspond to the 22 letters in the Hebrew alphabet. His research uncovered numerous additional parallels, including one between the Tarot and the Tree of Life. He became convinced that the Tarot was a compass, a means of circumnavigating the Tree of Life, becoming divine and wise, and eventually reaching the heavens.

A contemporary of Levi (Jean Baptiste Pitois, 1811-1877), the French occultist Paul Christian defined the Egyptian initiation ritual through his book The History of Magic (1870). According to Christian, the Giza Sphinx also served as a gateway to the holy vaults, where the Magi received their initiation. Corridors connected the subterranean portions of the Great Pyramid.

To assess a candidate's courage and intelligence, he was subjected to life-threatening ordeals. After passing these tests, the initiate descended the 78-rung ladder into a bottomless pit and discovered an overshadowed opening in a long gallery lined on each side with 22 statues and flanked by pairs of mysterious bodies and symbols. At that point, according to Christian, a magus named Pastophore ("guardian of the holy symbols") appeared to unlock the postulant's grating. "Welcome, son of earth," he said with a smile. You have escaped the pit by discovering the path to wisdom; only a few Mystery aspirants have passed this test; the remainder have been annihilated. As the great Isis is your protector, she will hopefully guide you safely to the sanctuary where virtue is crowned.

The Tarot evolved over time. Aleister Crowley, a famous British occultist, collaborated with Lady Frieda Harris in the 1940s to

13

create a Thoth deck that incorporated several different elements, including Jewish, Roman, Christian, and Islamic icons. Crowley began as a member of the Golden Dawn Order but eventually left to found his own order, the Silver Star, to represent his own unique (and erotic) occult brand.

Over the years, hundreds (if not thousands) of different Tarot decks have been created. The Tarot continues to evolve, despite the fact that its origins are unknown. And the Tarot's origins are perhaps less significant than what it is. After all, history is history. If the Tarot enables you to grasp your existence more fully, regardless of whether you believe in universal truth in the cards, all events preceding this realisation become meaningless, including, of course, the history of the cards themselves.

Numerous Tarot Packs

Tarot cards were originally an Italian pastime. However, it was verified through psychic readings. It is still one of the most frequently used instruments of worship in the Western world, and many people place their trust in the readings it has acquired. Numerous types of tarot cards exist, including the following:

The Ator: It has a new, energising aroma that is ideal for new-generation psychic readings. It has incredible stories and is well-known to a large number of people.

The Benedetti: Is lavishly decorated in gold leaf. It is the ideal choice for readers looking to add a touch of class and prominence to their offerings. They drew inspiration from the Visconti chips.

The Tarot of the Cat People: The cat people tarot is the best choice for those seeking a glimpse of a long-forgotten land. This demonstrates human ingenuity through mystics and animals.

Tarot Column Smith: Numerous mental readers have developed their visual literacy using an abstract paint approach. They are the ideal candidates for the column smith tarot. The mysterious tarot is the most obscure and rarely seen of the conventional tarot decks. It features strange characters that pique the interest of many. It is a relatively uncommon type of tarot card, as readers believe it has the potential to frighten consumers.

The Tarot de la Rose: This is a necessary skill for great thinkers. Historically, writers frequently referred to the ancient tarot.

The Swiss Foreign Symbol Tarot is accessible for a more satirical approach to tarot interpretation. It is a variant of their standard tarot reading.

For lovers of ancient writings, this tarot is a reference to one of the ancient writers.

Marseilles Tarot: The Marseilles tarot deck is widely available in a variety of shops worldwide for the highest level of divination among everyday people. Additionally, people used tarot to meditate.

The Minciante: Minciante tarot contains more than any other 97-card deck. The majority of people consider it to be one of the most popular games. The paladin tarot deck is ideal for modern tarot lessons. The ability is used in conjunction with standard tarot readings. It depicts elements of Egyptian classical sculpture, which are highly regarded by art enthusiasts. The phoenix tarot is designed for the twenty-first century tarot reader. It is a twentieth-century invention. It features vibrant colours and is thus quite eye-catching.

The majority of people seek tarot readings in order to forecast their life circumstances, fate, or disasters. Fear of the unknown fuels the tarot reading business. Tarot readers may use any of the tarot cards listed above to guide their actions.

The Importance of Truth and the Mystics Surrounding Tarot Cards

With over 600 years of tarot card experience, this ancient tradition has been associated with other intriguing tales, ideas, and facts. Some of them are true, while others are fabrications.

They are all fictitious.

The following are some critical skills you must acquire as a beginner or tarot card reader:

The current Tarot Deck contains 78 cards: 22 Major Arcana and 56 Minor Arcana. The readings of the large and miniature Arcane cards vary significantly; the names of the cards in the older set differed from those in the current tarot.

Significant Arcana as truncations, high priestesses as popes, hierophants as papas, coins, staves, or batons as weapons;

Tarot card decks come in a variety of styles. Each table features a unique image and description. The value of the tarot card remains constant across all decks; you can use a tarot deck called Birth Tarot based on your birth date. The cards have been customised through special tarot card readings based on the reduced number of your month, date, and year of birth; each card contains several images with varying meanings. Anyone can easily comprehend the meaning of tarot cards with the aid of a comprehensive tarot card guide;

Each minor arcane represents a specific aspect of life, such as cups, emotional obstruction, pentacles, financial and family difficulties, swords, trouble and conflict, walls, and ambition;

The major arcana cards represent significant breakthroughs, improvements, events, and life cycles, while the minor arcana cards represent daily life's difficulties and opportunities. Tarot readings are typically performed using other decks of cards called tarot spreads. This tarot diffusion describes and recognises a specific scenario, so the consumer frequently selects the appropriate tarot diffusion. Three types of readings are transmitted via Celtic Cross: True Love Reads, career path readings, and performance spreads.

Minor cards resemble playing cards. - the suit consists of fourteen cards, numbered from two to ten, and the five are knight, queen, king, as, and post;

The tarot card can be used anywhere there is a tarot deck or a device that reads tarot cards. To learn tarot cards, a beginner must choose a major mystic; without instruction or spiritual authority, anyone can read and learn tarot cards. All you need to do is follow your instincts and connect with the best tarot card guide.

Tarot Card Fundamentals

The origins of Tarot Cards are a matter of conjecture. Nobody knows for certain when the first decks of tarot cards were invented. According to some scholars, tarot cards originated in the 15th century, while others assert that they developed in the early 1300s.

Both acknowledge that tarot cards originated in Italy and were reimagined as "Tarocchi" cards for use as playing cards with no connection to divination or contemplation. Tarot cards became extremely popular in France during the 18th century, and the French pronunciation of "taro" with a silent "t" was universally accepted.

During the late 18th and early 19th centuries, a Catholic priest named Eliphas Levi used tarot cards in his mystical sorcery writings.

Levi was educated in a variety of languages (Hebrew, Jewish, Polish, Masonic, and Cabalist), as well as in a variety of scientific disciplines (Astronomy, Astrology, and Metaphysics). Levi honed his skills in a variety of languages. Levi created his own tarot deck as a teaching aid to assist his students in their studies of spiritual relationships and self-awareness. He was the first to incorporate the four elements of nature, astrological patterns, and biblical parallels into a tarot card deck. The use of these symbols has undoubtedly endured the test of time, with many new writers continuing to employ them.

The Rider-Waite deck, which was first published in England in 1910, is the most widely used tarot deck today.

Rider-Waite is a combination of the company's name (Rider Company of London) and the author's name (Arthur Edward Waite). In the late nineteenth century, an English mystic group called the "Hermetic Order of the Golden Dawn" became actively involved in tarot research. Arthur Edward Waite, one of his founders and leaders, was born in America and educated in England. He developed a series of tarot cards that could be used to forecast future events.

The Rider-Waite deck was revolutionary because each card depicted an image telling a story. Pamela Coleman Smith, another Golden Dawn designer, drew the cards. Her work influenced subsequent tarot artists.

Essential Components of a Tarot Deck

A complete set of tarot cards contains 78 cards. The Minor Arcana comprises 56 of the cards, while the Major Arcana comprises the remaining 22. Arcana translates as "hidden mystery." Arcana is a term that refers to deception.

Every day, the 56 Minor Arcana cards address significant and relevant issues. Additionally, they will be listed as 14 cards in four suits (Ace to 10, plus four court cards). Each suit is inspired by one of the four primary natural elements: fire, water, earth, and air.

Each fit is distinct in its own way:

The masculine aspect of Fire is represented by a tarot suit with'Walls' that represent behaviour, desire, energy, imagination, and spirit.

A tarot suit of'Cups' represents the feminine aspect of Water, evoking desires, thoughts, psychological abilities, and spiritual beliefs.

The masculine dimension of Air is symbolised by the tarot'Swords'costume, which represents clarity of thought, intelligence, creativity, and ideas.

The feminine dimension of the Earth is symbolised by the tarot suit of "Pentacles," which represents everything related to Earthly existence, the body, safety, and life.

Each suit contains fourteen cards, each with its own symbolic meaning:

- Ace: New Beginnings

- Two: Balance and Collaboration

- Three: Trinitarian Christianity, Sorcery

- Four: Establishment, Completion

- Five: Upheaval and Chaos

- Sixth: Perfection & Beautification

- Seven: Research and Spiritual Pursuit

- Eight: Infinity and Stability

- Nine: A Spectacular Number

- Ten: Harvest, Completion

- Pages dedicated to education and exploration

- Knights: Action, Movement

- Queen: Depth and Maturity - King: Strength and Power

The 22 Major Arcana cards address fundamental issues and intentions. The Major Arcana cards also tell stories about an individual's quest for existence and divine consciousness. Life experiences transcend the confines of time and space, as demonstrated by the Major Arcana cards. The trump cards are the largest cards in the Arcana.

The Tarot Cards' Utility

Tarot cards should be viewed as a tool for examining one's own existence and achieving a more positive outlook. The cards do not possess any mysterious powers and are unlikely to cause harm to you or others when used properly. Tarot cards should be used to acquire positive knowledge that can be applied to everyday situations and challenges. Tarot cards will reveal an increased sense of self-confidence, a fresh perspective, and a more nuanced understanding of your place in the world.

Numerous tarot readers have mentioned acquiring experiences that have aided in their comprehension of past events and ultimately enabled them to avoid repeating errors. Certain tarot readers use cards to forecast future events. Often, simply having an open mind to new ideas is sufficient to effect positive change in your way of life.

Tarot Deck Maintenance

On the website, you'll find a variety of helpful hints for maintaining your carts. Essentially, disinfecting the new card deck prior to its first use is recommended; this can be accomplished by placing the deck on a window cover for 24 hours to clean the cards of Sun and Moon.

After that, you should season your cards by sleeping with them under your pillow for a few nights. When not in use, the tarot should be wrapped in a velvet cloth and placed in a tissue (pouch).

How to Begin

To begin your journey as a tarot card reader, you must ensure that you have all of the necessary materials. The first item is a good guide, but this one can be crossed off the list because you are currently reading it. What else is there?

Your Very First Tarot Card Deck

There is some debate over how one obtains their first deck of tarot cards. According to some readers, the first deck a person owns should never be purchased independently. Rather than that, it should be given to them as a gift. Some go even further, stating that you should refrain from purchasing any of your tarot decks, whether they are your first, second, or fiftieth.

This belief stems from the superstition that purchasing your own deck will not only fail to work, but will also bring you bad luck.

This belief may have developed as the concept of tarot reading gained popularity and even those with no knowledge of how to read cards acquired a deck.

This, however, has been proven to be a myth by individuals who purchased their first tarot deck and did not encounter any bad luck or faulty decks. Additionally, it is critical for the success of your work that you use a deck that resonates with you. If you wait for someone to give you such a deck, you may end up waiting an eternity.

As such, I recommend that you do what feels right for you. If you prefer to wait for someone to offer you your first deck, that is an option as well. If, on the other hand, you wish to purchase it, the following guidelines should be followed:

Hold the cards and experiment with them prior to making a purchase. Your tarot cards should feel natural in your hands and be easy to manoeuvre.

Ascertain that you enjoy the illustrations on the cards and that they are easily identifiable. Examining your cards and liking what you see will add to the enjoyment of your job. Knowing which card is which makes readings much easier and smoother, and also gives the querent a positive impression of your work. This is not to say that you must immediately recognise each card: this takes practise. However, having a deck that facilitates that task is a good strategy.

Choose the deck based on the method of instruction you will use. The Rider-Waite one is ideal for those seeking as much information as possible, as it is the most popular and, as a result, has the most resources. Although in today's age, with the rapid growth of Internet usage, you can almost certainly find information on any type of tarot deck.

However, some are more subjective and leave the art of reading more open to the reader's interpretation, so if you are the type of person who typically learns through trial and error and by following your instincts, those decks may be a better fit for you.

Having said that, many experts argue that the Rider-Waite method is an excellent choice for beginners and that, once you gain a better understanding of taromancy, you can experiment with other decks and take on new tarot challenges.

Should You Purchase Used Tarot Cards?

This is another point of contention. There is no doubt that purchasing a used deck will save you money, as you will not be spending as much as you would on a new one (although there are new decks that are very low-cost).

Some readers argue against purchasing used tarot decks on the grounds that you can never be certain you're getting a good one. One card fewer or two duplicated cards renders your deck ineffective. You're always taking a chance.

As a result, the majority of card readers opt for new decks, allowing for the exception of rare or vintage decks (which can be more expensive than regular unused decks, and thus do not factor into this debate). Once again, my advice is to do what feels right for you as a reader at this point in your journey.

Your Tarot Diary

Every coin has two sides, and tarot reading is no exception. While each card has a predetermined meaning, there is also some subjectivity involved. Your journal is precisely what enables you to delve into the subjective realm of tarot and use your personal experiences to grow as a reader.

Every reader, in my opinion, should keep a journal from the moment they begin their journey into the world of tarot.

This way, you can confirm or refute your intuitions and gain a better understanding of the areas in which you need to improve.

Additionally, you can always look back and assess your overall progress as a reader. Because it is the most personal item you can keep from your learnings, this tarot journal takes on an emotional charge and will be something you enjoy looking back on in a few years.

Once you've acquired your tarot journal, the critical question becomes: what kind of information should you record in it? In short, you should write down everything that occurs to you during your practise sessions based on your personal experiences and interpretations.

Specifically, a few of those things would include the following:

Observations on tarot exercises. Again, exactly as in school! You will spend the first phase of your learning process performing exercises rather than actually practising the art form on other people. You're going to learn a lot of new information, possibly even things that weren't in your guide, so it's a good idea to jot them down.

Your interpretation of the card's meanings. As you conduct readings, you will notice that certain cards appear in situations where their traditional interpretation does not apply, but another interpretation, one that comes from your intuition, does. These newly discovered meanings for each situation are critical to record because they enable you to build your own "tarot dictionary." Additionally, these newly discovered meanings help to personalise your readings significantly more.

Tarot spreads, i.e. the arrangement of the cards that appear.

This is critical because each card position has a distinct meaning and, while there are established spreads that every card reader is familiar with, you can create your own layouts.

Mood-Setting Pieces

This is entirely optional, but many readers enjoy prepping the space in which they will practise tarot in order to make it unique to them and inviting to others. This may seem insignificant during the initial stages of learning the fundamentals of tarot; however, once you begin reading cards for others, you should devote time to making your tarot reading spot comfortable for both you and your client.

Candles, incense, sage, crystals, and pendulums are all items that tarot readers typically enjoy having. Some people prefer to listen to relaxing music in the background, while others prefer to keep a window open to allow the room's air to circulate. There are no rules about what you should purchase for your tarot spot; simply set it up in a way that radiates positive energy and an upbeat atmosphere.

Important Concepts to Understand

Tarot Card in the upright position vs. Tarot Card in the reverse position

You have already encountered the terms upright tarot cards and reserved tarot cards, but I have yet to explain the distinction between them.

When you flip a card and it lands upright in front of you, this card has significance (upright tarot card). However, it is possible for this card to land upside down, altering its meaning (reversed tarot card). While it may seem logical to assume that those meanings are mutually exclusive, as you will soon discover, this is not always the case.

Cards that are upright

The upright cards are the ones that every tarot reader is familiar with and uses. Before shuffle, those who read only upright cards ensure that each card in their deck is facing the same direction.

Reading these cards is much easier than reading the reversed ones, as they provide information on a more surface level.

This makes it easier to apply and adjust the upright pre-assigned meaning of the cards to the querent's specific question (s). This is also why it is recommended that new readers begin by learning the upright cards and then add the reversed cards to their reading sessions if desired.

Cards that have been reversed

Not every tarot reader reads exclusively reserved tarot cards. The primary reason for this is that reversed cards are frequently associated with negative readings (although, as you will see, this is subjective). Others believe that the 78 upright cards provide sufficient information for their reading sessions and that adding another 78 is unnecessary.

However, those who do read reversed cards reap the benefits; they add depth to your readings simply by providing additional information, allowing you to reach conclusions you might not have reached otherwise.

If you wish to incorporate reversed cards into your readings, all you have to do is alter the way your cards are shuffled. A good technique is to face all the cards in the same direction, then divide it (around 75% of the deck on one hand and 25% on the other), flip the smaller group of cards over, and thoroughly shuffle it.

After weighing the advantages and disadvantages of reversed cards, you must decide what course of action to take. However, I believe that you will never know for certain unless you give it a try, so even if you do not believe you will be a reversed card reader, consider doing so just once or twice.

It's also worth noting that sticking to upright cards does not make you a less skilled reader: it's your ability to interpret the cards and apply them to the client's situation that determines your skill level.

Your path as a tarot reader does not have to follow the same path; in fact, it most likely will not! If you decide one day to begin using reversed cards or to incorporate them into specific readings, that is perfectly acceptable. You should trust your instincts and do what feels right at the time.

Spreads of the Tarot

Thus, tarot spreads refer to the arrangements of the cards by the reader. This is a critical concept in the world of tarot because each position in these patterns imparts a unique meaning to a card, significantly influencing the reader's conclusions.

Numerous tarot spreads exist, which is unsurprising given that readers can create their own spreads.

However, some are more frequently used than others.

Astrology

Astrology is the study of the stars, the Solar System, and their effect on human moods and personalities. Thus, astrologers examine the positions of those cosmic objects at the precise time of a person's birth and deduce how they have shaped/will shape them as individuals.

While astrologists were once considered mathematicians, astrology cannot be considered a science, as there is no actual proof of a correlation between the position of cosmic bodies and a person's personality. Rather than that, astrology is frequently referred to as a metaphysical study, as it deals with subjects that are not scientifically verifiable.

We are all familiar with our zodiac signs and have read our horoscopes: these are based on the astrology assigned to those signs, and this is how the predictions are made! Individuals are assigned one of twelve zodiac signs based on their birth date, which are divided into four categories: Earth, Water, Fire, and Air.

Therefore, is there any relationship between astrology and tarot? Yes! Indeed, the two philosophies are inextricably linked in a variety of ways:

Both are based on the astral realm. Numerous tarot spreads created during the popularity of the Order of the Golden Dawn (an esoteric order with a strong emphasis on spirituality and astrology) are shaped like constellations. Each zodiac sign has a Major Arcana tarot card associated with it; Aries has The Emperor, Taurus has The Hierophant, Gemini has The Lovers, Cancer has The Chariot, Leo has Strength, Virgo has The Hermit, Libra has Justice,

CHAPTER 2:

GETTING ACQUAINTED WITH YOUR DECK

Selecting the deck

The tarot is made up of numerous symbols derived from a diverse range of human consciousness. All of the decks available are free to use and feature their own distinct set of symbols and system. Through the use of these symbols, you will construct your own personal narratives during your readings. Therefore, it is critical and more practical for you to select a deck that resonates with you. For the majority of beginners, the Rider-Waite deck is an excellent and simple place to begin.

If you are preparing your tarot cards, this indicates that there is information you require. The majority of people flee in order to find answers to the numerous uncertainties they are currently

29

confronted with. When used correctly, these tarot cards can assist you in seeing and considering alternative perspectives in order to move in the best possible direction.

Consider the information you wish to obtain from your tarot reading, such as "What is the best career path to take?" When reading the tarot cards, it's important to remember that the tarot is not a tool for predicting the future, but rather a tool for exploring your unconscious inner self. It is a means of projecting your hidden perceptions of things.

There are numerous Tarot decks available, but many practitioners prefer the Rider-Waite Tarot deck because they believe the energy emitted by each card is more discernible than in other card decks. Practitioners of white witchcraft and those who follow religions with naturalistic beliefs can consult the Tarot of the Old Path.

It is critical that you select a Tarot Deck that you feel comfortable working with. There are some superstitious beliefs that you should not purchase your tarot deck, but rather receive it as a gift from someone. It does, however, depend on your level of superstition.

Reading for your own benefit

Sacred Space Creation

One critical aspect of Tarot Reading is creating a sacred space in which to conduct your readings. The area should be free of disturbances and negative energies so that you have a better chance of connecting with your cards.

Ascertain that the location you've chosen is away from various city noises such as street noise, radio, karaoke, dog barking, or industrial sounds such as someone hammering, welding, or drilling.

Distractions from other people, things, or animals will obliterate the connection you are establishing with your cards as you read them.

When creating your sacred space, pay attention to your perception of how it should appear and your feelings about space, the Tarot cards, and your sense of spirituality, among other things. The decoration style varies according to the user; some may use crystals, plants, and silk scarves, while others may hang New Age art on the wall. Whatever path you take, ensure that it is consistent with your spirituality.

Cards should be shuffled and reset

While manipulating and shuffling your cards, you are actually establishing a physical connection with your deck. By incorporating your intuition into your reading, you can develop a strong connection with the cards. You may shuffle it once, or as many times as necessary to get the cards "cleared." By dividing the deck into thirds, you can rearrange the cards within the pack. When you are ready, face down these cards.

Tarot spreads provide a structure for exploring answers to your questions; each position of the cards in the Spread represents an aspect of your question. You are not required to include them in every reading, but they can be an excellent way to get started with your learning. The past-present-and-future spread is the simplest reading spread that can assist you in becoming acquainted with the cards. To begin, gradually reveal each card starting with the top card of the shuffled deck.

Give it a shot Try Utilization of the Three-Card Tarot Spread

With practise, you will gain confidence in your readings. Before attempting to decipher the meanings of individual cards, scan your deck and attempt to absorb any reactions you have to the images in front of you. Evaluate your emotions and how you feel about the objects, colours, and symbols if any. Keep these points in mind as you progress through the spread.

Obtaining Tarot Meanings from the Positions of the Cards

When you're first starting out, you'll need a reference guide to assist you. Typically, when you purchase a deck, it includes a reference guide. If you are unable to locate it using your Tarot card, consult online resources to assist you in locating meanings. We have included a reference guide in this book for your convenience.

To make sense of the cards in front of you, you must consider the meaning of the cards in relation to the question or query you are exploring. Tarot readings typically entail the interpretation of a random selection of events and their definitions.

Rituals are critical in the processing of events, and even if you are sceptical, treating your cards with respect and understanding their significance and value alters your perception of the world and its inhabitants.

Continue to be grateful as you read. Clear your cards at the conclusion of your activity and store them in a safe and secure location.

How to Practice and Fundamental Exercises

Now that you have the materials necessary to begin learning and are familiar with some of the fundamental concepts associated with taromancy, it is time to begin practising.

Before you begin reading for others, it is critical that you familiarise yourself with the cards, which can be accomplished through some exercises. When you complete these five exercises, don't forget to grab your tarot journal and jot down any pertinent information.

Five Fundamental Exercises Using a Tarot Deck

Exercise 1: Observation of Cards

The first exercise consists of four simple steps. The objective is for you to truly become acquainted with the imagery on each card and to discover what each one represents to you beyond its pre-assigned meaning.

Take a card from your deck and examine it for 30 seconds.

In your journal, jot down the thoughts that occurred to you during that initial observation.

Return to the card and examine it for a few minutes longer this time, paying close attention to the details in the illustration.

Create a story around the card. Fill at least one page of the journal, providing as much detail as possible about the story and growing in wisdom at the conclusion of each one.

There is no right or wrong answer to this observation exercise, as it is entirely subjective to your interpretation of each card.

Exercise No. 2: A Single Card, Numerous Questions

In your tarot journal, jot down five questions.

Take one card from your deck and shuffle it.

Utilize that card to provide responses to each of the questions you jotted down.

This will allow you to practise adapting one card and its pre-assigned definition to each situation. It is possible that you will struggle to find a way to use a specific card to answer a specific question, particularly on your first attempt. However, do not be discouraged. Take a break and come back to it the next day or even a couple of days later.

Negative Cards Exercice 3

Due to the fact that the interpretation of the cards is subjective, you may receive a negative vibe from some of the cards in your deck. This exercise enables you to investigate that sensation.

Consider all the cards in the deck and select the ones that elicit negative emotions in you.

Create a list of the reasons you believe that particular card makes you feel that way. This can be as simple as associating the illustration's colours with a particular bleak emotion or as complex as the card reminding you of a traumatic experience from your past.

Consider the flip side of the coin: in what circumstances might this card actually mean something positive?

Connecting a Card to a Friend or Family Member

This exercise assists you in comprehending the characteristics of each card by associating them with someone you know in real life, which can be an excellent way to help you memorise the card's key points.

Take a tarot card from your collection.

Make a note of the card's name and who it reminds you of; this could be a friend, a family member, or even a coworker. Make a note of why you made that connection and what the card and the individual have in common.

Exercise 5: Tell the story of your life using the Major Arcana Cards.

This fifth exercise will require additional time and commitment, but it has the potential to create an even stronger bond between you and your deck. This is where you will create your own Fool's Journey (i.e., the story told by the Major Arcana's 22 cards).

Consider the most significant events in your life, both positive and negative, and what has most shaped you during your time on Earth.

Examine your cards and associate them with the various stages you've experienced. You are not required to use every card; simply choose the ones that make sense.

Tarot Card Reading: A Step-by-Step Guide

You will eventually begin reading the tarot cards. You should begin by applying that process to yourself, noting in your tarot journal where you can improve and any pertinent thoughts or feelings that arise during your practise. This will expedite the process and will also help you determine whether you are ready to begin reading other people's tarot or if you still require additional training.

After practising on yourself a few times, try reading for someone close to you. It must be someone with whom you are completely comfortable; otherwise, you may not give it your all during the reading, adversely affecting your performance.

Following this, and assuming that is your goal, the time has come to begin performing readings for strangers and possibly profiting from them.

This is a significant leap, and it is critical that you do not rush your educational journey to reach this point. Tarot readers do not enjoy a favourable reputation, and there are numerous sceptics. You should not begin reading for strangers solely to earn money: you will become just another scam, and it will not benefit you in the long run.

Therefore, take that step only when you are ready and confident that you have accumulated sufficient knowledge and practise to make each reading session count. Each client should leave their session feeling as though their money was well spent and that they gained knowledge that will assist them in resolving a particular issue in their lives.

Now, regardless of whether you are reading tarot cards for yourself, a loved one, or a stranger, the process of reading tarot cards involves at least seven steps. At the very least, because some readers create their own rituals, which may necessitate additional steps. For the time being, I recommend that you stick to these seven. You may eventually feel the need to add some of your own, but this will come naturally.

As is customary, bring your tarot journal with you whenever you conduct a reading.

1. Adopt the proper mindset

It is critical that you prepare yourself mentally prior to the reading and that you are in a position to accept and decipher whatever the cards reveal. A simple but effective technique for establishing the proper mindset is to perform some simple but mindful breathing exercises.

While you're doing it, you can ask for guidance or visualise everything that's bothering you evaporating from your body as you exhale. As your practise progresses, you can also add a personal touch to this first step by saying a mantra that resonates with you, lighting incense, or listening to calming music.

2. Inquire about something specific

When you are ready to begin, it is time to pose the question. What do you require assistance with? What are you hoping to learn at the conclusion of this reading?

As a beginner, you should attempt to ask specific questions so that you can more easily examine a card and discern what your intuition is communicating. The more specific the question, the more easily you will understand how the card relates to it. You will eventually be able to address more general questions. To illustrate, a specific question might be "Should I accept the new job opportunity that has been offered to me?" while a broader one might be "How will accepting this opportunity affect my life?"

3. Reshuffle your cards

I recommend that you read only upright cards during this first phase, so shuffle your cards as you would any regular deck. Because many decks are larger than standard playing cards, it may take some time to master the technique. However, practise does indeed make perfect! After you've mastered the basic technique of shuffling your tarot cards, you can progress to more complex techniques.

Shuffle your cards to remove any residual energies from previous readings, which is critical for the current one to be as accurate as possible.

4. Destroy the deck

The way the deck is cut is determined by the spread that will be used for the reading. For your initial sessions, stick to a straightforward two-card spread:

Arrange your shuffled deck face down on the table.

Divide it into two piles and arrange them on the table next to one another. According to some, you should use your left hand because it is closer to your heart and is controlled by the right side of your brain. Others argue that you should do it with your non-dominant hand because you have less control over that hand and are therefore less likely to use your conscious mind to influence the process. As with many other decisions you will face during your tarot journey, I recommend that you choose the hand that feels right to you.

Once you've created these two piles, flip the top card from the right pile over.

5. Take note of your initial reaction when you see the card.

Now the reading begins in earnest. When you first saw the card, what did your intuition say? In your journal, jot down some key words that came to mind as you turned over the card and discovered which one it was.

6. Examine the card in greater detail

After you've recorded your initial impression of the card, it's time to examine it more closely. Take note of the colours, shapes, characters, and action taking place. Make a list of how each of those things makes you feel and how they might be connected to the question.

7. Bring the tarot reading to a close.

You should not conclude a reading session by simply putting the deck away and going about your daily activities. A few things you should always do are reshuffle your deck, express gratitude to your cards for the guidance they provided, and carefully repackage your deck, taking care not to damage it and ensuring it is properly protected.

This is another step in which you can develop your own rituals, such as a concluding mantra or some mindful exercises.

CHAPTER 3:

BEGINNING THE MINOR ARCANA

While it may be tempting to devote all of your time to studying the Major Arcana cards, given their vast numerical advantage over the suit cards in the deck, collectively referred to as the Minor Arcana, the likelihood of encountering suit cards in any spread is quite high.

Within a spread, the Major Arcana cards can be given greater weight or viewed as more critical to the ultimate interpretation; you could think of them as major plot points within a story, whereas the Minor Arcana cards comprise sub-plots and contextual histories. Nonetheless, the Minor Arcana cards cannot be overlooked or disregarded; they assist in translating the Major

Arcana cards' meanings from abstract concepts to useful and specific advice for the querent.

Fortunately, there are some tricks you can use to decipher the meanings of the Minor Arcana's fifty-six cards that will save you the trouble of memorising them all. Regardless of the style of the deck, whether it features unique illustrations or purely abstract designs, each Minor Arcana card will have a suit and number. Each suit corresponds to an element, and each number has its own significance. Even novices can make sense of a suit card by combining them without having any preconceived notions about its meaning.

Suits

The Minor Arcana is divided into four suits: Cups, Wands, Swords, and Pentacles. Each suit contains fourteen cards: an ace, a two, a three, a four, a five, a six, a seven, an eight, a nine, and a ten, as well as four Court Cards.

Bear in mind that the suits may be defined differently in different decks, particularly older ones. Historically, because tarot cards were used under the oppressive rule of the Roman Catholic church, which would not condone symbols of paganism, mysticism, or the occult, a suit of coins would typically be found in a tarot deck in place of pentagrams, and a suit of staves, batons, or even polo clubs would be much more likely to be found in place of wands.

The Cups Suit

All of the cards in this suit have a connection to the element of water.

They are largely analogous to our constantly changing emotions, feelings, and relationships.

The Wands Suit

This suit is associated with the element of fire and is symbolic of action and passion, both of which are both creative and destructive in nature.

The Swords Suit

These cards are associated with the air element and symbolise intangible concepts, truth, intellectual conflict, and physical, moral, or mental anguish.

The Pentacles Suit

This suit is associated with the earth element; previously represented by coins rather than pentagrams, the cards deal with practical matters such as finances, work, home, the body, and the necessities of life (sustenance, shelter, and safety).

How to Interpret Suit Card Numbers

It's critical to remember that these interpretations apply to all of the deck's numbers, not just the suit cards; these interpretations do not have to be applied to the Major Arcana cards, but with additional study of numerology, Tarot readers can gain a deeper understanding of all cards.

Additionally, the direction of these cards and their placement within a spread can have an effect on their meaning. For instance, while the Four card is typically associated with stability, when reversed, it may indicate the polar opposite, referring to volatility or a shaky foundation.

Alternatively, if an upright Seven card is typically associated with difficulty or adversity, a reversed Seven may indicate that something the querent anticipated being difficult turns out to be quite simple.

Numbers

The Ace, or number one, card represents a new beginning or a new beginning. It could refer to an opportunity, a new relationship, or the birth of a child.

Duality, division or union, choice, and dichotomy are all represented by the Two card. It could be a sign of interpersonal conflict, forks in the road, mirror reflections, or repetition.

The Three card is associated with creativity and expansion. While reproduction, or birth, is an obvious example of this, it can also refer to artistic creation, building, or personal development.

The Four card represents steadiness, strength, and a firm foundation.

It frequently makes reference to institutions like schools, churches, and even family units.

The Five card is associated with a state of flux, conflict, or difficulty. Consider someone who feels like the fifth wheel on a double date; their presence adds tension to an otherwise comfortable, stable, and predictable situation.

Harmony, peace, balance, and contentment are all associated with the Six card. Additionally, it can allude to abundance, fulfilment, and satisfaction.

The Seven card represents a difficulty, obstacle, or struggle.

In comparison to the Five card, this one indicates a more complicated issue that does not have an easy solution. While the Five denotes an uncomfortable state that prompts change, the Seven denotes an ongoing struggle that prompts introspection.

Consider Five as a representation of institutional or group problems, whereas Seven refers to a personal problem for the querent.

The Eight card is symbolic of works coming to fruition, manifestation, accomplishment, and fulfilment. Additionally, it can denote forward momentum, progress, and satiety. It is not only a symbol of success and positivity; it can also refer to situations that the querent previously identified as disasters waiting to happen, which ultimately result in disaster.

The Nine card is associated with both positive and negative endings; it can represent either successful completion or devastation in the form of loss. In either case, it typically refers to an outcome that results in some form of isolation (each Nine card in the Rider-Waite deck features an illustration of a lone figure), increased awareness of oneself, and reliance on one's own strength, wisdom, and resilience.

The Ten card also speaks of endings, though it does so in a more permanent and conclusive manner than the Nine card does. It may symbolise the ultimate manifestation or culmination of work, completeness, or finality. Consider the Nine card as representing the negative or pessimistic side of an ending, whereas the Ten card represents the positivity and optimism of a new beginning; think of Nine as representing the grief associated with loss or death, whereas Ten represents the promise of rebirth.

By combining suit and number, a formulaic interpretation is possible.

Novice cartomancers can get a sense of the meanings of numbered suit cards by combining the suit and number significance of the card. Consider the following examples.

Cups Two - The number is symbolic of duality, union or division, and freedom. The suit is symbolic of emotion and love. When these elements are combined, they point to a loving relationship or a strong emotional connection between two people. The spread's context and the querent's prompt will assist the reader in determining whether these references refer to a romantic, platonic, familial, or professional relationship.

If the card is upright, it indicates a positive development in the relationship; if it is reversed, it indicates division, conflict, or a split.

The Four of Swords - The number four is symbolic of stability and fortitude. The suit is symbolic of intelligence and conflict. By combining these concepts, we can deduce that the card represents intellectual fortitude or mental stability, possibly in the face of adversity or difficulty. The true meaning of the card expands on this interpretation; by reading the illustration of the card, which depicts a figure laid to rest in what appears to be a church, we can deduce that this card indicates an extended period of involuntary thought and introspection, most likely prompted by physical incapacitation. This is precisely why beginners will benefit more from illustrated decks such as the Rider-Waite Tarot than from a deck with abstract designs for the numbered suit cards.

Seven of Wands - The number seven represents conflict and difficulty, while the suit connotes passionate action and creative energy. When these two concepts are combined, we see that this card represents an individual who is willing to roll up their sleeves and tackle a problem, willing to think outside the box in order to find a solution, and willing to work diligently to repair whatever is broken. Additionally, it may imply bravery in the face of danger.

Nine of Pentacles and Ten of Pentacles - Both numbers denote completion in some way; the Nine refers to an individual's end, while the Ten denotes the culmination of all efforts. In this instance, the suit represents practical concerns such as finances, physical health, and values. Thus, the Nine of Pentacles card may represent someone who has finally earned enough money to afford a vacation, retreat, or day of self-care; whereas, the Ten of Pentacles card may represent a windfall or jackpot, company bonus, or lottery winning. The Nine of Pentacles represents an individual pausing to enjoy the fruits of their labours, whereas the Ten of Pentacles represents a group accomplishment that results in abundant rewards for all parties involved. Again, the illustrations on these cards assist in making the distinction clear.

The Court Playing Cards

Court card titles vary significantly between decks. While the Rider-Waite deck includes a Page, Knight, Queen, and King for each of the four suits, Crowley's Book of Thoth deck recasts them as a Princess, Prince, Queen, and Knight, in the order of their respective status. In older historical decks, the Page is occasionally referred to as the Knave. Numerous modern decks aim to use gender-neutral titles for these cards or to invert traditional gender norms, such as by making the Queen the highest status card or by replacing all four characters with female titles. Regardless of their titles or genders, each Court Card is intended to represent an archetypal character or personality type present in the querent's life.

There are several different ways to read the Court Cards, which is where the reader's personality, experience level, and intuitive ability come into play. Numerous experienced cartomancers agree that the Court Cards typically represent specific people or archetypal characters in the querent's life. Interestingly, the Tarot deck contains sixteen Court Cards, which appear to roughly correspond to the sixteen Myers-Briggs Personality Trait Indicator (or MBTI) personality types—though this is far from an exact science, and opinions on card-MBTI correspondences vary.

While the Court Cards are typically depicted as detailed characters with distinct features, it's important to remember that they represent distinct personality types that can take almost any physical form. A Queen of Cups card could easily represent a male in the querent's life, just as a King of Swords card could easily represent a female.

Perhaps the simplest way to grasp the Court Cards is to consider them as formulaic combinations; each is defined by its suit's element, rank or status, and masculine or feminine energy.

The four suits correspond to the four elements: air represents swords, water represents cups, fire represents wands, and earth represents pentacles or coins.

Additionally, each rank is associated with one of the four elements: Kings are associated with air, Queens with water, Knights with fire, and Pages with earth.

Control is the elemental energy of air. A person ruled by the air element is typically intelligent, philosophical, and eccentric; carefree, optimistic, and endearing; they may also be self-sufficient, selfish, and callous.

Water's elemental energy is perceptive. A water-ruled personality can be intensely emotional, compassionate, and intuitive; merciful, passive, and adaptable; kind-hearted, introspective, and selfless to an extreme; but also fickle, irrational, and deceptively powerful.

Fire's elemental energy is action. Someone ruled by fire is typically courageous, passionate, and charismatic; creative, adventurous, and courageous; lustful, irritable, and volatile; and occasionally violent and destructive.

Earth's elemental energy is acceptance. A person ruled by the earth element is typically practical, level-headed, and rational; emotionally stable, consistent, and responsible; respectful, humble, and occasionally a little dull-spirited; receptive to learning, and willing to put in the effort necessary to accomplish goals.

Additionally, we can correlate the Court Card ranks to a person's level of maturity or experience. This is not a literal age reference; the elderly can be quite childlike, while the young can be wise beyond their years.

Additionally, we can connect the Court Cards' masculine and feminine identities to their yin and yang energies. The masculine Court Cards (Kings and Knights) are active and assertive, whereas the feminine Court Cards (Queens and Pages, even if the Pages are depicted as men) are passive and receptive.

Consider the Page of Pentacles. The Page's rank corresponds to the earth elemental energy (practical, rational, eager to learn, accepting); his rank also implies that he is inexperienced, with a youthful spirit; and finally, while he is depicted as a man in the Rider-Waite deck, the Page's rank corresponds to feminine energy, implying that he is passive and receptive. Thus, even without knowing his attire, we can deduce that this character is likely a diligent worker and, due to his inexperience, a dedicated learner, receptive to whatever wisdom the universe has to offer. Because the Page's suit is Pentacles, or Coins, which is frequently associated with financial matters, we can view him as a student or entrepreneur on the verge of success. He is a sign of impending good fortune, and he is capable of receiving and putting it to practical use.

Additionally, you can strengthen your grasp of the court cards by encapsulating the above formula within the suit element. For instance, the King of Cups possesses elemental energy as defined by his rank (King=air), a high level of maturity or experience as defined by his rank, and a tendency toward assertiveness as defined by his gender. Typically, when we consider this formula, we envision a powerful individual who is arrogant, impulsive, and perhaps even insensitive and selfish. However, when we consider the suit element's influence on this formula, we see that this personality exists within the context of water; this strong, experienced, assertive personality is influenced by emotion, intuition, introspection, and passivity. Thus, the King of Cups can be interpreted as a mature, authoritative, and courageous individual who has chosen to use his (or her) power for the greater good of love, compassion, and selflessness.

These formulas are always useful for cartomancers who prefer not to rely on strict memorization or rigid definitions of cards, as they allow for a great deal of reader discretion and intuition. Without illustrations to guide them, readers may struggle to grasp the subtleties of the cards' meanings or easily lose track of the contextual implications affecting the card's interpretation.

The Cups Suit

Each card in the Suit of Cups is associated with the element of water and is associated with emotions, love, relationships, compassion, and intuition. While the Suit and its associated element are typically regarded as feminine, this does not preclude these cards from representing men or non-binary individuals.

In any spread, it's critical to remember that the cards in this suit represent emotions, not necessarily behaviours or objective truth. For instance, a querent seeking guidance in a romantic relationship may become discouraged upon receiving the Five of Cups and Seven of Cups, both of which imply a change of heart and conflict, as well as the reversed Two of Cups, which imply a choice and division. When taken together, these cards indicate a schism in the relationship. Perhaps a lover is tempted to abandon their partner in pursuit of a new love—that seems the most logical interpretation, doesn't it?

However, the reader should recognise at this point that these cards are all from the Suit of Cups and may represent feelings rather than actions. If none of the other cards in the spread indicate infidelity or an impending breakup, it is entirely possible that these cards are highlighting the querent's fear of losing their love to someone else. They may be cautioning against self-fulfilling prophecies; if the querent fears adultery and allows their fear to influence their behaviour, they may unintentionally drive their lover into the arms of another. Alternatively, these three Cup cards may indicate that the querent's partner is physically committed to the current relationship but is having difficulty integrating it with a change of heart in another area of life: for example, the querent's partner wishes to relocate to a new home on the other side of the world but is unsure how to do so while maintaining the relationship. This story is equally at home as a story of temptation and faithlessness as it is with the three aforementioned cards.

Finally, depending on the total number of cards in your spread, you may want to keep track of the number of cards laid from each suit. If the spread is overwhelmingly dominated by upright Cup cards, this can indicate that the querent will need to connect deeply to their emotional body and trust their intuition moving forward, regardless of the situation or prompt. This could also indicate that the overall outcome will be determined by emotional reactions rather than rational thought or practical judgement. By contrast, if the spread is dominated by reversed Cup cards, this may indicate to the querent that their emotions about the current situation are ultimately irrelevant, or that emotion is impeding progress and resolution.

Always keep in mind that context is critical.

Ace of Swords

Upright - A new emotional beginning; a new love or the progression of an existing relationship to a new level of intimacy; creativity.

Reversed - Blockage or repression of emotions; unrequited love; creative stagnation.

Symbolism - This card depicts a hand emerging from a cloud, a representation of divine gifts. In its upward-facing palm, a single cup represents the Holy Grail—the ultimate symbol of love, devotion, and creativity. Above it, a dove is dropping a communion wafer into the chalice; the dove represents hope, peace, and healing, while the wafer symbolises transformation. The hand and cup float above a pond filled with lotus flowers; lotus flowers are a symbol of rebirth, growth, and beauty.

Two of Cups Standing - Mutual attraction; committed relationships; intense love (romantic, platonic, or familial); stable union.

Inverted - Discord; schisms, splits, and breakups; conflict; miscommunication; self-absorption; discord; schisms, splits, and breakups.

Symbolism - Two figures (a male and a female) stand opposite one another, each with a cup in one hand and a free arm reaching for the other. Above them, between the cups, is the Caduceus symbol, which alludes to Hermes' staff; it is also a modern symbol for western medicine, implying the healing powers of love. A winged lion's head atop Caduceus represents passion, courage, justice, and majesty.

Three of Cups Upright - Joy and celebration; playfulness and creativity; gatherings and collaborations; attitude of "the more, the merrier"; sharing happiness and spreading love; supportive community.

Reversed - Overindulgence; literal and metaphorical hangovers; broken friendships and disjointed social circles; a yearning for solitude.

Symbolism - Three women dressed in brightly coloured robes dance in a circle, each cup raised high in the air. They are adorned with floral wreaths that symbolise victory and accomplishment. They are surrounded by grape vines, fruits, and a pumpkin, which all symbolise a harvest, the reaping of rewards, and bountiful divine gifts.

Four of Cups Upright - Introspection and solitude; emotional inaccessibility or withdrawal; apathy; disinterest; narrow-mindedness; rejection.

Reversed - A renaissance; seizing opportunities; optimism, openness, and zeal.

Symbolism - A young man sits at the base of a tree, his arms crossed across his chest and his gaze directed downward. His body language indicates that he is not open to giving or receiving love at the moment. Three cups are lined up in front of him and remain untouched, possibly indicating that he has already emptied them or that he has no interest in their contents. A fourth cup is presented to him by a phantom hand reaching through the clouds—a divine gift!—but he does not appear to accept it.

Five of Cups Upright - Sadness, heartbreak, loss, regret, disappointment, anguish, sorrow, and grief.

Reversed - Self-forgiveness; acceptance of losses; surrender; letting go of the past and moving forward.

Symbolism - A lone figure dressed in a black mourning cloak stands with his back to us, staring down at three spilled cups on the ground, either oblivious to or willfully ignoring the two upright cups behind him. There is a castle in the distance, on the other side of a river, and a bridge connecting them, symbolising long-term goals and the fact that this tragedy will eventually fade from memory; everything becomes water beneath the bridge.

Six of Cups - Adolescent attitudes; pleasant strolls down memory lane; nostalgia and joy.

Reversed - Stuck in the past; harbouring grudges; rigidly adhering to traditions with no room for experimentation, playfulness, or innovation.

Symbolism - Two children are playing in a garden adjacent to a house; the older boy offers the younger girl a cup containing a blooming flower. The house behind them is a symbol of stability, security, and safety. A guard patrols the city behind them, protecting them from external dangers and allowing them to play freely. Flowers are symbolic of youth and growth.

Seven of Cups - Decisions and choices; wishful thinking; lofty ambitions; daydreaming; abundance of opportunities.

Reversed - Importance of choice; if you do not make a decision quickly, you risk losing all of your opportunities.

Symbolism - A figure stands with his back to us, in front of him are seven cups, each with a different symbol spilling over: a face, which symbolizes either youth or love; a castle, symbolising security and power; a wreath, representing victory; a snake, representing intrigue or temptation; a wyvern or dragon, standing for wrathful power; a pile of golden coins, symbolising wealth and riches; and a shrouded figure with arms splayed wide, signifying spiritual enlightenment.

53

These seven options may correlate to each of the seven deadly sins referenced in the bible.

Eight of Cups Upright - Satiety, exhaustion, or boredom; walking away or moving \son; abandonment, escapism, and wanderlust.

Reversed - A return; inability to let go; giving it one last shot; overstaying your welcome; biding time.

Symbolism - Eight cups are stacked upon a shoreline as a solitary figure ventures off, walking stick in hand, leaving the cups behind.

The moon hangs overhead, a symbol of fluctuation and the cyclical nature of change. The figure seems to be heading towards mountains in the distance, implying that they are ready and eager to tackle challenges; change is often an uphill battle, but in this instance, difficulty is preferable to the sense of ease, comfort, and boredom being left behind.

Nine of Cups

Upright - Personal success and satisfaction; contentment; wealth and luxury; self-care; wishes fulfilled.

Reversed - Be careful what you wish for because you might get a whole lot of it; overindulgence; dissatisfaction; desire as a bottomless cup.

Symbolism - A man sits with his arms crossed and a broad smile on his face; nine cups are lined up in a row behind him on an altar.

His crossed arms indicate that he has met all of his needs and is not in need of anything else; his smile indicates that he is content; and his feathered cap attests to his ambition, hard work, and well-earned success.

Ten of Cups Upright - The rewards for which you have waited your entire life; true love; blessings; triumph; return home; joyful unions; alignment, coincidence, and synchronicity; bliss; spiritual fulfilment or nirvana.

Inverted - Ignored connections; misalignment and misunderstandings; familial and romantic discord; profound social schisms. This can also refer to the sensation of having everything you've ever desired and still feeling unsatisfied or incomplete.

Symbolism - A family stands beside a river on a grassy plain, beneath a rainbow of cups. Each parent has one arm wrapped around their child, while the other reaches up to the sky in gratitude and appreciation. The rainbow is a representation of majesty, beauty, and divine blessings. The collective stance of the parents demonstrates both romantic and spiritual love. Their two children dance joyfully alongside them, symbolising innocence, hope, new beginnings, and the concept of coming full circle.

Upright Page of Cups - The page is inexperienced and inexperienced, but he is acutely attuned to his emotions and intuitions. He is imaginative, inquisitive, romantic, empathetic, naive, and idealistic. He aspires to spread a message of love, truth, and joy. This card represents new beginnings and new relationships.

Inverted - Hypersensitivity, immaturity, and an unwillingness to reason.

Additionally, this reversed card may indicate an inability to listen to or honour one's intuition.

Symbolism - The page stands with one hand on his hip and the other on a chalice with a fish peeking out from beneath the brim. As with the crayfish in the Moon card, this fish represents subconscious knowledge rising to the surface from the murky depths. Take notice of your inner voice!

Knight of Cups Upright - This character may have been the inspiration for your favourite fairy tale's Prince Charming. He is romantic, noble, courageous, and immensely charming. This card is not simply about love; it alludes to a romantic journey or spiritual quest, as the Knight's rank is associated with active energy and youth. He's making a name for himself and winning plenty of hearts in the process.

Reversed - The reversed Knight of Cups evokes the sensation we have when something that seemed too good to be true turns out to be a complete nightmare. On the surface, the Knight appears to be perfect and ideal, but beneath the surface, there is jealousy, anger, moodiness, and emotional instability. This reversed card represents a break with reality or an illusion that conceals an unpleasant truth.

Symbolism - The Knight rides a white horse, a representation of his intention's purity. He offers a cup. He wears a winged helmet, which alludes to Mercury, the divine messenger; this indicates that he has a silver tongue and is capable of charming anyone with the beauty and eloquence of his communication style. He directs his gaze straight ahead, his spine as straight as a rod; he appears to be aware that he is being observed and admired.

Queen of Cups Upright - This card embodies the pinnacle of emotional equilibrium. For a lifetime, the Queen of Cups has benefited from her intuitive and emotional sensations. She is now seasoned, an authority and expert on matters of the heart and soul. She possesses clairvoyance, creativity, sensitivity, emotional maturity, and a natural ability to heal. Her compassion shines like a beacon, drawing others to her energy, inspiring them, comforting them, and eager to accept her advice and guidance.

Reversed - Too much of a good thing can be extremely detrimental; this is true of emotion, intuition, and creativity. When this card is reversed, it indicates that a person who had the potential to be compassionate and emotionally mature has developed into melodramatic, manipulative, obsessive, or dishonest. Most likely, they've lost touch with their empathetic drive as their own extreme emotions and desires have surpassed their ability to perceive the needs and feelings of others. This could indicate extreme narcissism masquerading as love, or it could indicate codependency.

Symbolism - The Queen is depicted seated on a throne at the sea's edge. She is crowned with jewels and holds an enormous and ornate cup adorned with crosses, crescent moons, grapes, and other symbols; this cup represents spiritual wealth or divine wisdom. She carries the universe's secrets in the palm of her hand. Her throne is adorned with seashells and cherubs who gaze lovingly and admiringly upon her; she is cradled by both the sea and the heavens.

King of Cups Upright - This card combines the rational and intuitive faculties. The King of Cups is an enduring symbol of love, even after lust and novelty have faded. He embodies dedication, compassion, benevolence, diplomacy, and peacemaking. He also embodies well-managed sensitivity; he is acutely aware of his emotions but never allows them to overwhelm him or motivate rash, volatile behaviour.

Similar to the reversed Queen of Cups, this card indicates emotional instability and manipulation, but with a more assertive tone. The reversed King of Cups may be using coercion or emotional blackmail; he may be drowning in his addictions and unable to see through his emotional fog. He can also represent someone who imagines himself to be a powerful authority figure, oblivious to his own emotional immaturity and imprudent behaviour.

Symbolism - The King sits on his throne, one hand holding a cup and the other holding a sceptre. He casts a serene gaze into the distance, implying emotional fortitude. He is alone, however, with his throne perched on a floating platform in the sea; in the distance, a ship passes and a fish leaps from the water. The ship is a representation of navigation, whereas the water is a representation of emotion and the subconscious. The leaping fish is symbolic of the ascension of emotions and intuition to the surface. The grey stone platform on which his throne is perched represents stability and fortitude.

The Suit of Wands Wands, like the other suit items (Cups, Wands, and Pentagrams), appear in the Major Arcana illustrations as well, held by the Magician and the princely warrior in his Chariot; the woman on the World card holds two!

Wands are associated with manifestation, creation, passion, and action in Tarot. They exemplify raw energy, ambition, willpower, and transformation. The Suit of Wands is associated with the element of fire, which, like the Suit of Wands, represents passion and energy, but also sexuality, volatility, expansion, release, and purification.

When the Suit of Wands dominates a spread, it indicates that the querent should concentrate on transforming possibilities into realities.

Wands are the tools we use to project our thoughts and ideas into the external world, and when a Tarot spread contains a large number of them, it's likely that the universe is beckoning you to step up and create something. The Wand functions similarly to a microphone and speaker box; it amplifies and projects what is already within you, allowing your unique mind to manifest authentic creations bearing your unmistakable signature. This means that you do not have to be a creative type to answer the Suit of Wands' call; you can start a business, start a family, or start a spiritual practise if these options make more sense to you than painting, writing, or dancing. The point is innovation and invention; this suit is not geared exclusively toward artistic endeavour.

The Wand is associated with a mysterious energetic life force known as Qi, or Kundalini, in non-western metaphysical healing practises such as Reiki and Tantra Chakra work.

This life force is a form of vitality that animates and propels all living things toward their individual destinies. All of the cards in this suit can be interpreted as a summons from the universe; now is not the time to rest on your laurels or become bogged down in overthinking things.

You are prepared to solve problems, generate new ideas, connect people, and carry out your plans. Concentrate on a single objective, grasp your wand, raise it high in the air, and manifest, manifest, manifest!

Ace of Wands - Ace cards are frequently associated with new beginnings, and this card is no exception. This card represents the beginning of a new creative endeavour or business venture; it represents inspiration, invention, and opportunities that are simply too good to pass up.

Reversed - This typically indicates that, even if your latest project began strongly, it has stalled, lost steam, or petered out. Distraction; procrastination; setbacks and delays; indecisiveness; and insufficient planning.

Symbolism - A divine hand extends from the clouds, holding aloft a sprouting wand. Some of the leaves are falling to the green earth beneath, where trees are growing—this represents new possibilities and the germination of seeds. A river and a castle on a distant hill are visible in the background. The river symbolises movement and momentum; the castle symbolises stability and security, but it is quite a distance away, implying that in order to create, you may need to embrace instability and become comfortable with vulnerability.

Two of Wands - Success in the short term; taking the first step in the right direction; planning and progress; discovery and accomplishment.

Reversed - Do not hesitate; if you act quickly, you can still take advantage of this excellent opportunity, but the window of opportunity is rapidly closing. This card may represent a lack of planning, self-doubt, futile anxiety, or fear of risk.

Symbolism - A cloaked man stands on a balcony, one hand clutching a long Wand (technically a staff) and the other a globe.

Behind him is another staff, planted in the ground and capable of standing on its own. He casts a longing glance over the trees, grass, water, and distant mountains. The fact that he is holding one staff while planting the other indicates that his initial success has only fueled his ambition; he is ready to move on to the next venture. The balcony's walls represent security, stability, and comfort; he gazes beyond them, indicating that he is beginning to wonder if these things are actually restraining him rather than protecting him. Is now the time to take a chance?

The globe he holds in his hand alludes to the adage "The world is your oyster." Everything he requires is at his disposal; all he needs to do is seize the appropriate tools and take a courageous step forward.

The Three Wands

Upright - Expansion; travel; forward momentum; stepping outside of one's comfort zone.

Reversed - Acclimating to life as a large fish in a small pond; stagnation; failed plans; travel difficulties.

Symbolism - A man stands on the precipice's edge, facing away from us, gazing out over the sea and distant mountains.

He is dressed similarly to the Magician in the Major Arcana.

He stands in front of three planted staves, each representing a previous accomplishment; with his hand on one, he sets his sights on the next leg of his journey. In the distance, a few ships are sailing. He may be awaiting the arrival of a shipment, or he may be preparing to board one and sail away.

Upright Four of Wands - A celebration of hard-won rewards; relaxation; stability; harmony; joy and relief.

Reversed - Continuing to be optimistic, but with diminished joy; tainted happiness; something dampens your celebration.

Symbolism - We see a party from afar; in the foreground of the card, four tall Wands are planted, and floral garlands are strung between them to form a canopy. This indicates victory—a hard-fought and well-won battle! Women dressed in floral wreaths dance behind it, bouquets of flowers held aloft; behind them, a castle stands as a symbol of security and authority.

Five of Wands Upright - Competition; creative tension; conflict; a test or rite of passage; sportsmanship, sparring, performative debates, or physical combat.

Reversed - Confronting inner demons; healthy competition devolving into viciousness; passive aggression; conflict avoidance; breaking rules in order to win.

Symbolism - Five male figures fight with their Wands, which appear to be Swords. However, some of them are smiling, and none of the Wands are aimed directly at them. This is a playfight, and several of the players have not yet mastered the art of wielding a fictitious sword—one character holds it over his shoulder like a baseball bat, while another thrusts his Wand straight up into the air. This is an example of a competition serving as a learning experience.

Upright Six of Wands - Victory; public recognition; optimism; confidence; victory within reach.

Reversed - Embarrassment; betrayal of success expectations; a fall from grace; a failed endeavour; a declining leader; private recognition; an unnoticed personal victory.

Symbolism - A male rides through a cheering crowd on the back of a white horse wearing a yellow cloak. The man is dressed in a red cape. The horse's colour denotes sincerity; the yellow cloak denotes optimism; and the red cape denotes boldness and passion.

He is wearing a floral wreath and is holding another wreath at the end of the Wand he is holding in his hand—this indicates a significant victory.

Seven of Wands Upright - Overcoming obstacles on your own; perseverance; personal fortitude and resolve; standing up for what is right; facing numerous adversaries or challenges alone.

Inverted - Weakness and exhaustion; loss of determination; cowardice; defeat.

Symbolism - A figure stands on the precipice's edge, facing the ledge. Six of the Wands in the card are threateningly pointed at him; he grips the seventh with both bands, not as a Sword, but as a shield across his torso. He wears a shoe on one foot and a boot on the other, which may allude to indecision, but also to the value of distraction tactics or the character strength required to stand out from the crowd and break the mould.

Eight of Wands Upright - Quick action; rapid progress; endeavours nearing completion; rapid change; air travel.

Reversed - Delays and detours; stagnation; intense frustration; resistance to change.

Symbolism - This is one of the few cards in the Tarot deck that does not feature a single human figure. Eight wands soar through the air, about to touch down. Their proximity to the earth represents culmination or manifestation; what was previously intangible and airborne will soon become a physical reality.

Nine of Wands Upright - Faith that has been put to the test; goals that are just out of reach; last-minute setbacks or curveballs; resilience and persistence;

Inverted - Failure; despair; loss of faith; defensive attitude; an individual pushed beyond their limits; broken or unacknowledged boundaries.

Symbolism - A figure stands in front of eight of the nine wands, peering over his shoulder at the others as he leans on the ninth. He appears exhausted and is wearing a bandage on his head. The bandage is symbolic of a head or ego wound.

He's come so close and yet he may not make it; he risks becoming too dejected to complete this project, despite the time and energy already invested.

Ten of Wands Upright - Strenuous labour; bearing the world's weight; extreme burdens; final push to complete a major project.

Reversed - Relief; delegation; implosion under pressure; completion; release; relinquishment of responsibilities.

Symbolism - A man holds a bundle of ten Wands in his arms and charges forward towards a distant house. He is constructing something, and it is nearly finished—but is his eagerness to complete it causing him to bite off more than he can chew? He looks down at his feet, and the Wands obscure his view of the distant house; he is so focused on forward momentum that he is unaware of how long this journey is, and that he may not complete it without assistance.

Wands Page

erect - The Page of Wands is passionate, inventive, vivacious, and endearing. Additionally, he is impulsive—a thrill seeker who is unafraid of risk or danger. He is brimming with novel, innovative ideas and is passionate about the pursuit of knowledge. He is a free spirit who will not be restrained or caged in; he is constantly moving forward and upward!

Reversed - When immaturity is combined with boldness and a desire for adventure, it can be a dangerous combination. Inverted The Page of Wands is impulsive and rebellious. He desires to share his creative energy with the world and blames others for impeding his potential; what he fails to recognise is that he is the one impeding his own emotional growth.

Symbolism - The Page stands alone with his Wand as a walking staff, his gaze directed upward, implying lofty ambitions and a daydreamer's attitude. He wears a feather in his cap, which is typically a sign of achievement or victory in battle— but given his inexperienced rank and lack of connection to warfare, this feather may indicate that he has a chip on his shoulder or an exaggerated sense of personal capability.

Knight of Wands Standing - The Knight is mounted on a galloping horse and is engaged in an unrelenting pursuit. He has his sights set on the prize and possesses the bravado and confidence necessary to persuade obstacles to leap out of the way. He evokes an adventure, a risk taken, or an unwavering pursuit of a goal.

Additionally, he embodies impulsiveness.

Reversed - Apply the brakes; while your mind and heart are prepared to take on this challenge, you may have forgotten about your physical or financial limitations. This card implies that inexperience, as well as a lack of planning and preparation, can result in mission failure. Additionally, it can imply an explosive temper, recklessness, or destructive impulsivity.

Symbolism - On an auburn horse, the Knight gallops ahead.

His helmet is adorned with bright red feathers, symbolising the passion that propels him forward.

CHAPTER 4:

BASIC TAROT INTERPRETATION TIPS

Often, when people begin practising tarot, their approach is rather simplistic–they learn the definitions of the various decks, select a few, arrange them in a pleasing pattern, and create a cogent interpretation. It is not until you delve a little deeper into the tarot system that you realise how intricate it is. Here are some suggestions for evaluating taro meanings and developing your readership.

1. Acquaint yourself with the Basic Definitions

Surprisingly, I've met a number of people who believe that understanding the meaning of each card is superfluous. We gently suggest to me, "Hey, I'm intuitive; I don't need to know all of this."

66

Perhaps this is because it can work for a truly gifted individual. They are, however, few and far between. This aids in the comprehension of a popular tarot deck. In other words, the underlying meaning of the card is identical. Then familiarise yourself with the fundamentals.

2. The Initial Reactions

Never lose sight of your initial emotional response when confronted with a card.

It is always true. Unfortunately? Disappointed? Additionally, conduct thorough research on the document. Scary? Scary? Verify ALL of the words—many of you are taken aback.

3. Examine the Photographs

Understanding a deck implies that we take photographs for granted. Each time, attempt to view them with a new perspective. You must develop the ability to apply the image to the problem in this manner. Consider how each person has arranged their cards. Are they communicating with one another? Turning our backs on one another? Averting your gaze? Avoiding each other's gaze? How about the climate? How about the climate? What colour does heaven appear to be? Are the trees being whipped by an autumn gale? How might this affect the interpretation of the card?

4. Conduct a Pattern Analysis

Do you anticipate seeing the same card in subsequent tests, even for others? And be aware that you, the listener, are considering it. Take some time to examine the token more closely—it holds personal significance for you. What happens if three or four cards of the same value appear—and don't forget to include Majors as well? Why might the number five rule be applicable in a lecture? Or how about the three Queens? What does this potentially mean for your customers?

67

Even if the majority of the available cards are blades or cups? How would this affect the card's perception?

5. Embrace Elemental Dignity

Primordial Dignities, as illustrated by Paul Hughes-Barlow on his blog Super Tarot. This is an enthralling subject that explains how suits assist or obstruct one another. For instance, in a three-card reading in which two Cups and one Wand appear, fire is subdued by water (emotions). The Wand card is weakened, regardless of its strength.

6. Utilize Numerology

Understanding divine numerical development is always beneficial in tarot analysis. In the preceding tip, I mentioned more than two cards numbered five (including the hierophant), indicating that the individual is seeking a large number of challenges, or even a major challenge that overshadows all other aspects of his life. If the result card is a ten, the current phase has concluded and another reading is necessary. Understanding your numbers will significantly assist you.

7. Identify the narrative thread

Each card in the tarot deck, even a single card reading, tells a story. Certain cards may reveal a more complicated story, and it is your responsibility to locate and pull the string. It can be challenging until you've completed a substantial amount of reading. I've found that involving the client helps — they frequently provide a clue almost accidentally. Celtic Cross is an excellent narrative.

8. Maintain a journal

If you have an insight, a revelation, or learn something new about your card, jot it down. Whenever you experience difficulty hearing, jot it down. Believe me when I say that these brief remarks will prove extremely beneficial to your future self. Utilize a tarot book to read, document, and evaluate.

9. Recognize the Archetypes

Major Arcana is centred on archetypes–fundamental forms found in all cultures and societies that date all the way back to Plato's time when they were first described. Numerous experiments have repeatedly demonstrated that they are a valid concept. The tarot's archetypes represent the stages of life through which we all pass. There is insufficient space for this fascinating subject, but as a tarot reader, you would be wise to assimilate some archetypal information. You may never have to discuss them in class, but familiarity with the Majors can significantly enhance your perceptions.

10. Symbolism

Each tarot deck carries a distinct symbolism. An icon is a pictorial representation of something else (think traffic signs) that you are unaware of. Numerous tarot images have been based on extremely dark myths or metaphysical concepts. Several of the more prevalent ones, such as colour, the presence of birds, plants, and livestock, are worth investigating.

11. Traditional vs. Modern Tarot readers of yore had a unique perspective on the meaning of the tarot cards. Additionally, it was contingent upon which occultist wielded the greatest influence at the time. Obviously, things change from time to time, and thus some of the older connotations have no place in the modern lexicon. Nonetheless, it's fascinating to travel back in time and compare old and new, so set aside some study time to do so. It's always beneficial to have an additional layer of meaning.

12. Inquire About Your Own Life

Your life experience improves as you age. If a card or a set of cards triggers a memory from your own life, draw on your reading experience. You are not required to demonstrate the root to your consumer.

Similarly, previous readings may reappear.

Numerous human experiences are universal, i.e., other people have had similar experiences to yours. Take care when a memory bubble appears—it is critical.

Whether you incorporate one or two of these concepts into your tarot analysis or all of them, your success as a reader can increase with each level of understanding. Never cease to learn; never cease to know.

How to Utilize Clarifying Cards

The final card indicates what you should do or refrain from doing in order to avoid loss. This indicates the direction you can take if the card is favourable or serves as a warning if the card is unfavourable.

For those who choose to encourage the cards to run, clarifying cards can provide additional information and details during reading. Additionally, we can raise certain concerns and assist you in comprehending cards that are merely incidental.

Naturally, many writers employ clarifying markers. Others use it solely to refine a forecast, gaining additional knowledge about how the card may refer to a particular situation if it becomes uncertain.

Due to the fact that each card can have an infinite number of interpretations, clear-cut cards enable the user to determine which meaning(s) is preferable.

Here are a few of the techniques I employ. None of them are methods I learned from a book or a teacher; they were all developed organically over the course of more than two decades.

Consider how they work for you and how you can incorporate them into your own strategies!

1. Use a clarifying card to explain a particularly perplexing card. When you see a pointless card, speak quietly to the player and inquire, "What are you attempting to communicate to me?" or "Who are you speaking to?" and take another card from the stack. Next to the ambiguous card, place the clarifying card. Determine whether the clarifying coin provides an answer to the question. What happens when the clarifying card definitions are combined with the original token?

2. Use a clarifying coin to delve deeper into the subject. If the card has already addressed your query, but you require additional information, ask a more specific query.

3. Create a second, smaller spread with a different deck to achieve clarity, specifics, and key points. Avoid interfering with the initial spread. Pay special attention when you see the identical coin!

4. Inquire specifically about the reading, such as "What is the best way to do this?" "How should my mentality behave?" "How can I be assisted?" or "What is the divine purpose?" Draw a card or a small card to represent a query.

5. To summarise the read, spread the final card: not every speaker or user must be addressed. However, if you believe these strategies are sound, experiment to see what happens. You might

be surprised at the amount of information and consistency that you
can obtain!

CHAPTER 5:

TAROT RITUALS

The rituals performed here are not those depicted in films, in which participants must draw mysterious symbols on the ground, dress in hooded robes, place candles in specific locations, and then begin reciting incantations while waiting for a huge, frightening gust of wind to blow. As fascinating (or terrifying) as that would have been, tarot reading does not involve any form of fetish ritual. In this context, 'ritual' refers to a series of actions performed prior to a tarot reading in order to help calm your mind and 'activate' your intuitive abilities.

To survive in the real world, you must constantly analyse how much money you have spent on gas, how many years you have left to pay off the mortgage, how many calories you have consumed in a day...the list is endless. However, to conduct an effective tarot reading, you'll need more than your analytical mind; you'll also need your intuitive mind. The rituals are simply a way to assist you in clearing your mind and allowing your intuition to guide you through the reading.

It is critical to understand that performing a ritual is not a necessary condition for an effective tarot reading session. If you believe you can use your intuition effectively without first preparing your mind, then by all means do so. However, over the centuries, the majority of people have found it extremely beneficial to have a specific routine that prepares them to engage their intuitive abilities prior to conducting a tarot reading.

Preferably, your ritual should be a recurring practise. It can be as simple as taking a few deep breaths and closing your eyes to help you calm your mind, or as complex as using velvet, silk, crystals, candles, and incense to create an atmosphere that you feel helps you connect with your mind's deepest recesses. There are no specific standard procedures for tarot rituals. It's all about determining what works best for you and maximising its effectiveness in order to establish a delicate balance between your analytical mind and your intuition. Once you feel that delicate balance has been achieved, you may begin your tarot reading session.

It is critical that your ritual procedure is composed of steps with which you are completely comfortable; both mentally and physically. If you are allergic to something, it makes no sense to use it if you believe it will bring you peace. If something scares you, it makes no sense to incorporate it into your ritual routine. You want to be calm, not apprehensive, as you conduct your tarot reading.

However, as long as you are comfortable with a particular sequence of steps, proceed. Even if it's simply carving specific symbols in the sand, lighting candles, and reciting whatever incantations come to mind, as long as the ritual process brings you peace and activates your intuitive abilities, fire on.

Prayers comprise a sizable portion of the majority of people's tarot rituals. If you believe in God or the existence of a supreme supernatural entity, you can seek guidance and direction from Him as you prepare to seek answers to your burning questions. Communicating with an unseen divine entity not only helps to calm you down and strengthens your intuition, but it also enables you to remain composed enough to frame your question properly. When you pray, you are likely to state your question aloud; to seek God's assistance. As a result, prayer assists you in framing your question precisely and without ambiguity.

Another critical component of most rituals is determining how many times you will shuffle the tarot deck prior to conducting your reading.

The number of times you shuffle the deck will eventually have a direct effect on the outcome of your reading, so it is critical that you remain objective when deciding how many times the cards should be shuffled.

75

While preparing your mind to conduct the reading, it is critical for you to decide whether you will shuffle the tarot cards alone, with the querent, or with the querent alone. As previously stated, there is no one-size-fits-all method for performing these tasks; it all comes down to personal traditions and, of course, intuition. While performing your ritual, it makes sense to mentally visualise the tarot reading in advance and determine who will perform the card shuffling.

Numerous tarot experts believe that during the reading process, a unique, ephemeral, and mysterious bond exists between the deck of cards, the reader, and the querent. The open-minded environment helps to connect them, and as the reader and querent open their minds to the possibilities of the reading's results, they discover themselves subconsciously cooperating to solve the querent's problems.

CHAPTER 6:

ENHANCING AND EXPANDING YOUR TAROT READING PROWESS

Tarot is a form of art. Regardless of how many spreads you master or how many card meanings you memorise, there is always another step you can take to improve your practise and understanding.

Establish goals and intentions for your readings to ensure continuous improvement. Keep a Tarot journal to track your progress and remain open to experimentation. Your progress may not always be linear, direct, and forward-facing; you may need to take one step forward and then back a few steps to re-examine concepts you previously believed you understood completely but now see deeper layers or hidden complexities within. There is no shame in unpacking and relearning the fundamentals you already know.

Male and Female

Additionally, you can read spreads while keeping an eye out for the balance of feminine and masculine cards; does this spread, as a whole, lean toward assertive, active, and rational? Or is it more emotional, passive, and receptive? Alternatively, you could focus on elemental energies; upright and reversed cards; or you could even read Minor Arcana cards as changing circumstances, while Major Arcana cards refer to life's constants or immovable realities.

Tarot and Astrology

Numerous Major Arcana cards feature symbols from the zodiac signs, which are inextricably linked to our understanding of the four elements and the four suits that reflect them.

Astrology is a highly complex science, with vast amounts of data available for interpretation. Begin by incorporating astrology into your Tarot practise. The following is a list of the twelve zodiac signs and the Major Arcana cards to which they are connected, as well as their associated elements. Aries - The Emperor - Fire

Gemini - The Lovers - Air Taurus - The Hierophant

Cancer - Water - The Chariot

Leo - Fortitude - Fire

Libra - Justice - Air Virgo - The Hermit

Scorpio is associated with death and water, while Sagittarius is associated with temperance and fire.

78

Capricorn - The Devil - Earth Capricorn - The Devil - Earth Capricorn - The Devil

Pisces – The Moon – Water Aquarius – The Star – Air

The remaining Major Arcana cards are associated with individual planets or celestial bodies rather than with entire constellation signs.

Mercury - The Magician - Air Uranus - The Fool - Air

The Moon of Earth - The High Priestess - Water

Venus - The Empress - The Continent

Jupiter - Fortune's Wheel - Fire

Water - Neptune - The Hanged Man

Mars - The Tower - The Flamingo

The Sun of Earth - The Sun - Fire

Pluto - Retribution - Fire

Saturn – The Earth – The World

There are additional astrological correlations for each numbered suit and Court Card, which can become overwhelming complex without a firm grounding in astrology. Study the twelve zodiac signs, their seasons, and the personality traits associated with them; this knowledge can assist you in making sense of perplexing spreads, identifying specific characters as representations of real people, and incorporating a sense of timing into your predictions.

Seasons and Suits

If you're feeling overwhelmed by Tarot's astrological associations, one way to simplify the concept is to group the zodiac signs according to their houses, or seasons, and then correlate those to the four suits. This enables some readers to forecast timing in a reading, for example, informing their querent that the resolution to their issue may not occur until the following winter season. Some readers are uncomfortable using the cards in this way because seasons repeat—they may be wary of raising someone's expectations for the coming autumn when the cards are pointing to an incident that will occur during the autumn season several years from now, or even during the figurative autumn season of one's life (middle age). In that case, the seasonal implications of suits can be used to enhance the mood of the ensemble. Summer cards can convey a sense of ease, carefree attitudes, and emotional closeness. Autumn cards may connote the brisk winds of change or the harvest season's sense of manifestation. Winter cards may allude to conclusions, endings, and death, whereas spring cards may allude to rebirth, survival, triumph over adversity, and moving on.

The suits and their associated seasons can also be linked to the four corners of the earth, though opinions on these connections vary considerably among cartomancers. They each have a corresponding colour.

Spring - Fire - South - Yellow - The Suit of Wands

Summer - Water - West - Red - The Suit of Cups

Autumn - Earth - East - Green - The Suit of Pentacles

Winter - Air - North - Blue or indigo

Numerology and Tarot Numerology is the study of the symbolic meaning and symbolism inherent in numbers.

This method can also be applied to the Major Arcana cards, governing the relationships between cards within a spread. For instance, in a spread that includes the Fool, the Magician, and a Ten of Wands, the Major Arcana's numbers one and zero could be associated with the Ten card, implying that all three cards are connected by a narrative arc or theme. A spread dominated by the number ten indicates culmination, finality, and conclusion, and because so many of these cards feature wands, you may conclude that a creative endeavour is about to pay off handsomely.

Although the number zero is not used in the interpretations of Minor Arcana cards, it is extremely significant in numerology and the Major Arcana. It denotes an absence of responsibility, expectation, and constraint.

This study heavily relies on addition, multiplication, and division. If you're interested in incorporating numerology's theories into your Tarot practise, it's prudent to first study numerology independently, and then merge the two methodologies.

Geomancy and Tarot Geomancy is another intricate and ancient form of divination. It refers to the physical alignment (or lack thereof) of objects or lines in space. The term "geomancy" is derived from Latin, ancient Greek, and Arabic roots, which mean "foresight of the earth" or "sand science."

Geomancy is exemplified by Feng Shui, as well as tasseography (the art of reading tea leaves), crystal scrying, the I Ching, Kumalak, and even rune casting. The earliest Geomantic methodologies, according to historical evidence, originated in Africa, or possibly in ancient Arab civilizations; these methods employed handfuls of dirt thrown into the air and analysed the patterns in which they fell, or,

81

alternatively, lines and dots drawn in the sand with the sharp end of a stick.

Cooking, Crystals, and Creativity

If astrology, numerology, and geomancy leave you perplexed, numb, or stressed, it may be time to return to the lighthearted and carefree side of Tarot.

Crystals can assist in lifting the mood of your Tarot practise and protecting your deck from negativity. And, what's more, they're gorgeous! You might want to begin collecting crystals with the intention of creating a sacred space or altar in your home; they can be extremely beneficial for meditation, yoga, reiki, and chakra healing. Additionally, they can be used in crafts or worn as jewellery.

As adults, we often forget how we spent our days as children; without work, taxes, dating, commutes, errands, or other adult responsibilities, the majority of us were forced to be resourceful and learn to entertain ourselves. We used our imaginations to run wild as we played pretend, with or without toys and costumes.

Tarot cards and crystals can both be viewed as toys designed to stimulate adult play. Bring your inner child to life. Disregard the rules. Do you gravitate toward a crystal for its metaphysical properties or simply because it is sparkly, pretty, and makes you feel good to hold it? Perhaps the latter, but who cares! Do you require a more compelling reason?

Attraction is a fundamental form of intuition; therefore, strive to put an end to your doubts about your impulses and desires. It is entirely possible that you have a valid reason for liking certain things. Whatever crystals (or bones, petrified wood, dried herbs, essential oils, or other organic materials) you are drawn to could be divine inspiration. Lean into that pull; honour, respect, and allow it to guide you.

To infuse your Tarot practise with some carefree fun, you might want to experiment with using the cards as a source of creative inspiration. Several simple examples include cooking, painting, and creative writing.

Shuffle your deck and draw cards at random to inspire your next steps—whether that's the ingredients you use in a recipe, the colours or shapes you choose for a blank canvas, or the characters and plot developments you use to advance a fictional story.

Additionally, some people find Tarot cards beneficial for free-writing (writing for the sake of therapy, as opposed to writing to create a complete narrative arc). Whichever path you take, you'll be amazed at how easily Tarot can reinvigorate your creative drive, assisting you in thinking outside the box, innovating, and bypassing artistic roadblocks.

CHAPTER 7:

MEDITATION AND MINDFULNESS WITH TAROT

There is a reason that the game of tarocchi became so popular that it evolved into the modern Tarot: each card, from the Page of

Pentacles to the powerful Hierophant, is layered with meaning, energy, and magic. During meditation, tarot cards make excellent focal points for manifestation. Here are a few methods and cards to get you started.

The Magician's Personal Power

It's natural to feel down on oneself at times in life, as if other people have taken your power. When we wonder how to reclaim our power, it can be extremely frustrating to the point of distraction. To begin, power is limitless. You are not robbed of your power; rather, other people or circumstances drain it from you. What you require is a replenishment from the universe.

Before you begin your meditation, ensure that you are comfortably dressed and seated in a quiet location. If you are unable to sit on the floor, you may sit in a chair as long as your back is straight and your feet are flat on the ground, palms down on your lap. The card should be in plain view in front of you.

The Magician card is numbered One in the major arcana. Consider how you'd like the opportunity to begin again, on a new, uncharted path.

Consider the four elements symbolised by the cup, the sword, the wand, and the pentacle. Consider how your emotions, intellect, spirit, and ego are all brimming with vitality, strength, and energy.

Concentrate on the infinity sign. Allow the universe's infinite energy to replenish your personal strength and vitality.

Attaining Long-Awaited Objectives – The World Card

When you feel as if you've been adrift on a calm sea for an extended period of time in life, you can use this meditation to bridge the gap toward a goal you've desired for a long time. The

World card is all about accomplishment and the immense satisfaction that comes with long-awaited success.

To begin, visualise your sacred space being bathed in purple, healing light.

Purple carries tremendous energy as the vibration of psychic ability and intuition, as well as being the ancient royal colour of choice.

Consider the World card's connection to the Magician card—both feature the same wand. That is because it is your own personal strength that has propelled you toward achieving this objective.

Consider the sense of accomplishment and pride you will experience when you accomplish this goal. Consider how others will congratulate you.

Gently sense the energy of new beginnings unfurling within your spirit as you accomplish this goal; as one thing comes to an end, life's cycle renews it to begin something else in its place. This is due to the fact that growth and learning are limitless.

The Star and Healing

The Star is an excellent card to meditate with when you're feeling down or hopeless. It will serve as a focal point for your thoughts, and its straightforward, calming symbolism can help rejuvenate your spirit.

Concentrate on the seven white stars and remember that the number seven brings luck and the assistance of the divine feminine to assist you in overcoming your difficulties.

Following that, focus exclusively on the eight-sided yellow star. Eight brings comfort to those who are in financial difficulty or who are suffering from fatigue or hopelessness.

Concentrate on the life-giving water of the universe refreshing your soul as the figure in the card pours water onto the soil.

Permit yourself to let go of anything that is no longer serving you and make a commitment to honouring your body and spirit in the days ahead.

Equilibrium and Temperance

It's easy to become overworked, stuck in hyperdrive mode, unable to slow down, or otherwise fixated on the mindset of more in this fast-paced world. We purchase new items to make ourselves feel better; we eat and drink more in order to stabilise our volatile emotions. When you feel the need for a spiritual reset, spend some time meditating with the Temperance card.

To begin, concentrate on the embroidered triangle and square on the angel's robe. This is symbolic of the relationship between humanity and nature. Have you lost contact with your natural self? Sensitize your frantic spirit to the serenity and wildness of the world. Consider the sound of ocean waves lapping against the shore or the breeze rushing through a high mountain meadow.

Next, concentrate on the angel's halo crown. Bear in mind that you, too, are inextricably linked to the divine and the universe. Reconnect with your own unique spiritual journey. Nobody can impose this on you or take it away from you.

Inhale the fragrance of growing things, such as the daffodils and lush, green grass depicted on the card. Heal yourself through the gentle gurgle of a flowing stream.

Similarly to how the angel balances the water in each cup, visualise the balance within you reestablishing itself.

Finally, fix your gaze on the rising sun in the distance and feel your body and mind relax.

Meditation on Love and the Lovers Card

While most of us desire true love, it is frequently difficult to define, let alone find. The most effective method of discovering true love is to allow it to find you. How are you going to accomplish this? By preparing your spirit, heart, and mind for love. When you are truly receptive to love, it is obvious to everyone you meet.

Many of us have looked back on a failed relationship in retrospect and noticed something about how it began: on a whim, when we least expected it. What are the implications of this?

Simply put, love will come to us on its own terms, but we can be prepared for it when it does. We are prepared to receive it, to give it, and to honour it through our words, actions, and promises.

Concentrating on the figures in the card, recognise that true love never conceals anything. It is self-assured, respectfully true, and honourably authentic.

Recognize that love is a state of being, not a state of action. You choose to show up each day in love with your partner, regardless of how difficult or peaceful the day is.

To bare yourself to another, you must first come to terms with, and even love, yourself.

The best love is a union of the spirit, the heart, the mind, and the body.

CHAPTER 8:

DEVELOP YOUR INTUITION THROUGH TAROT

The Tarot can be a fabulous method to build up your instinct, Inner Wisdom, Higher Guidance or anything you desire to call it or give you the certainty to confide in your instinct. In a perfect world, you need to arrive at a spot where your instinct naturally kicks in at whatever point you need it and you don't need to consider it. You simply realize that something is correct or wrong and you confide in it totally. Tarot can likewise help you securely investigate potential alternatives before you concede to settling on a choice and can give you direction in any part of your life.

What Exactly Is Intuition?

It is a technique for acquiring knowledge or accessing data that is not immediately apparent to the five senses of sight, contact, hearing, smell, and taste.

This could be an indication that something is highly improbable and you should proceed with caution, or it could be a sense that something is ideal for you and you should feel free to do it. It could be a voice in your head, an image, or an almost instinctive response.

This could also be in reference to an individual and your ability to trust them.

It is frequently a first response and may appear to you to be quite unreasonable and silly at first. In any case, it will be mostly accurate.

Your instinct or premonition is always there to assist you.

Once in a while, your mind becomes so cluttered with chatter and your body with so many emotions that you are unable to hear, believe, or see your calm, all-knowing truth. It is critical to learn how to distinguish unhelpful personality babble from genuine Intuition.

Instinct is comparable to any muscle. The more you use it, the more effectively it will serve you and the more readily available it will be when you need it.

The Magnificence of Images

Your mind works in pictures, and the Tarot contains 78 colour images and pictures, many of which are antiquated, making it one of the most prevalent methods for legitimately communicating with your subliminal personality.

The most seasoned method of educating and learning is through images, as they recount stories and tap directly into the right side of your mind, which is concerned with innovation, creativity, motivation, thoughts, and bits of knowledge.

The more you can activate the right side of your brain, the more you can rely on your instinct or hunch.

The photographs, hues, and images speak directly to your subliminal personality, providing you with the responses that are most appropriate for you. This is why different individuals can interpret similar cards differently, as the cards address each individual individually.

Visuals, audibles, and sensations

When working with tarot cards to develop your intuition, it is critical to be aware of any sounds, voices, contemplations, feelings, images, or vibes that surface as you pose questions and examine the cards. These will almost certainly be significant.

Do you hear any words or voices when you look at a card? What is being said? What is the voice's tone and volume? Is it internal or external to you?

What emotions do you experience when you view the card?

Where are the emotions located in your body? – Is it the heart, the head, the legs, the stomach zone, the back, or something else?

Where have the photographs gone? - Before you, inside your head? Is it true that they are coloured or starkly contrasted, stationary or in motion?

Are any sensations present in your body, and if so, where are they located? Do any images streak through your mind?

Trust those initial responses; they are almost certainly correct for you.

Avoid looking at the card for an extended period of time, as your coherent personality will most likely begin to unravel and will most likely convince you not to acknowledge those initial bits of knowledge.

Once you've mastered the art of perceiving the sign that your instinct uses to communicate with you, you'll be able to tell them apart much more quickly in another situation.

With a little training, you can quickly recognise the appropriate responses from your instinct and your explanatory personality's rationale.

Both are critical, and the systematic personality can be extremely beneficial once all of your inventive bits of knowledge have been gathered.

When you are prepared, take a moment to relax, quiet your mind, and choose another card.

Activities for Developing Intuition Instinct will generally work in one of two ways: 1) to warn you of danger, so you avoid doing something or quit doing something; and 2) to alert you that a person or thing is great and will present you with a beneficial result.

At times, the emotions associated with Positive or Negative can be completely distinct and unmistakable. Occasionally, however, they can be difficult to recognise because you may be experiencing apprehension, which can be extremely close to fear, or your intelligent, diagnostic personality may have immediately intervened to warn you not to do something — for a variety of legitimate reasons – when that activity may actually be beneficial to you.

This may be the case if you have a strong desire to contact someone, as it may prompt something admirable, but you delay and do not pick up the phone out of fear for that individual's position, or out of fear that they will refuse to speak with you, or out of fear that they will dismiss you.

Occasionally, in order to capitalise on something great, you must venture beyond your usual range of familiarity and take a risk beyond what you would normally do; by that time, dread and rationality have become an integral part of the equation, and opportunities can be missed. The fear is frequently that the activities will not result in the desired increase but will instead result in torment, misfortune, and suffering.

A natural streak can, and almost certainly will, occur at any time, and the message is not entirely obvious. This is why it is critical to be aware of how intuition appears, sounds, and feels to you in both positive and negative situations.

I'm sure you've encountered situations throughout your life in which you had a premonition or a natural blaze about a person or thing.

You will occasionally have tuned in to it and followed your intuition, regardless of how illogical it appeared. At various points, you may have overlooked it and pursued what appeared to be an increasingly rational strategy.

I would venture to say that on the occasions when you followed your intuition, you were correct and this resulted in a positive outcome; on the other hand, on the occasions when you ignored your intuition, things did not come together as they should have.

Instinct is not synonymous with "premonition," as your body appears to know exactly what is correct or incorrect for you.

The following are two or three activities that will help you reconnect with your instincts.

This will also assist you when you are posing questions to your cards and expecting prompt, dependable, and accurate responses.

We'll examine the sights, sounds, emotions, and sensations associated with admonitions, as well as those associated with beneficial things.

These will be unique to each individual due to their unique recollections, circumstances, and affiliations. The activities are designed to assist you in utilising your own triggers, so that you eventually understand what they are really after.

Connecting with your Intuition

The most important activities to complete for your Intuition to attempt to caution and energise you are those in which you listened to your Intuition, took action, and experienced a positive and awesome result.

In any case, be aware that your psyche may hurl instances when you ignored your Intuition and things went wrong for you. Avoid using these activities as a means of self-thumping, as that is not their intended purpose.

If your brain brings up negative memories for you, I've included a few activities to help you cleanse the negative feelings and feelings associated with them.

Exercise One – Recognize when your intuition is warning you

This is a mindfulness exercise, not a time to dwell on the past, particularly if you believe you committed an error or have whipped yourself over it since.

You have probably encountered instances throughout your life when your Intuition attempted to warn you of danger, to convince you not to believe someone, or to warn you that something terrible might happen. If you listened to your Intuition, you most likely felt fantastic afterwards, especially if things worked out well for you.

If you ignored the alerts and things went wrong, you may still harbour feelings of blame, fault, lament, or recrimination toward yourself or others.

If negative thoughts and feelings or agonising recollections arise as you consider Developing Your Intuition, it is critical to clear them before you begin, as they can impair your ability to tune in to your instinct. The polar opposite of what you need is an unhelpful voice whispering in your ear, saying things like "remember what happened the last time we attempted to caution you."

You can use some of the Clear Limiting Beliefs sound unwinding that is included in this bundle to dispel pessimism, or perhaps it is more beneficial to simply return to a position of harmony with past events and errors of judgement.

If that is the case, you may benefit from tuning in to the Acceptance Audio Relaxation, which is accessible through my website.

Your Higher Guidance is not filled with resentment. It does not stop providing you with useful information simply because you have overlooked it or are not tuned in to it.

Recognize Warnings

Take a deep breath, quiet your mind, and consider a time in your past when your instinct attempted to warn you about an antagonistic person or thing.

This should be a two-part activity. One is the location where you tuned in to your Intuition's admonitions, and the other is the location where you did not tune in.

You may choose to recall either scenario. Generally, it makes no difference.

Reintroduce yourself to the situation. Make an attempt to recall being in the situation, seeing who else was there, hearing what was said, and seeing what was happening.

You presumably made a choice or made a move at some point during that experience. Return to the guide ONLY PRIOR TO deciding on that option. Take note of any sights, sounds, voices, feelings, bodily sensations, or anything else that may have changed subtly in a moment. This is your Intuition attempting to connect with you in order to warn you against moving forward or managing the individual in front of you, or about something that was harmful to you in some way.

Bear in mind that this occurred in a split second and would have been extremely difficult to discern in the moment it occurred. Alternatively, perhaps you did not miss it and responded unexpectedly when you heard or felt the instinctive prompts.

Reconnect with those sights, sounds, emotions, and sensations that existed PRIOR to the choice and make an attempt to truly see them. What kind of people were they? Which part of your body did you encounter them? Is it true that it was a vision or a flash of impending doom? Is it true that the voice was raucous? If it was a voice, what tone did it have that caused you to pause and reconsider your choice?

From my experience, voices warning of danger will generally be uproarious, clear, and direct, frequently mentioning your name.

Did you overhear something else? If you were at home, your entryway ringer may have begun to ring or your telephone may have abruptly rang.

My friend revealed to me that when she met new people at networking events, she would hear a voice in her head clearly say "NO" when the individual would not be a good fit for her to start a new business with.

The voice was always direct, as she discovered a couple of times when she failed to hear it out!

Did your body give you an indication that something was wrong? If that was the case, what was it? Where had it gone? Numerous individuals report feeling prickles running up their backs or experiencing a chilling sensation. What did it accomplish for you?

If you disregarded your Intuition's warnings, did you receive a prompt voice or sensation of "Ought not to have done that or ought not to have said that?"

The more grounded your instinct is, the easier it will be to spread it in order to use tarot cards to augment natural knowledge. Following that, we'll discuss how to use tarot cards to develop instinct.

You could then repeat this activity with another memory to determine whether the sights, sounds, voices, emotions, sensations, and encounters were equivalent in an alternate scenario in which your Intuition was attempting to warn you.

Try it in a situation where you were managing someone and your instinct warned you that they were dishonest or that something bad was about to happen as a result of the experience. Once again, you can examine instances in which you tuned in or did not tune in and your intuition was validated.

This is not a judgmental activity; this is a perceptional activity. If these recollections have elicited negative emotions, such as lament or recrimination, it is critical to engage in some clearing activities to separate and release that energy.

Elimination of Negativity

If negative feelings and recollections rise to the surface as a result of this activity, it is critical to STOP and CLEAR them immediately.

You might want to try the following as Quick Energy Clearers:

Wave your arms and cut a triangle around yourself from the crown of your head to the soles of your feet, as if you were cutting up negative energy and releasing it into the Universe.

Make use of St. Germain's Blue Flame. Consider remaining inside a blue fire of light that is purifying and transforming anything negative into positive energy.

Utilize Acceptance's sound reflection to relinquish the negative passionate charge associated with an event and view it objectively as "what is" or "what was." The occasion occurred, and while that cannot be changed, your feelings about it can.

To clear negative energies, wave a lit sage stick around.

Inhale deeply and expel negative emotions into the Universe.

Take a deep breath and as you exhale, expel all the air from your lungs and then snicker profoundly as Ho, Ho, Ho to expel significantly more old, stale air from your lungs.

CHAPTER 9:

TIPS TO ENSURE A GOOD READING

1. Creating a Harmonious Environment

Believe it or not, the environment in which you read tarot has a significant effect on readings. Not only can the world have an effect on you as a tarot reader, but it can also have an effect on the story. It is always necessary to set aside personal issues and concerns when reading tarot. The creation of a comfortable room that allows you to remain focused and relaxed can assist you in remaining rational and objective while reading. Additionally, rituals such as candle or incense burning will help you get in the mood.

2. Choose a Card as a Signifier

Significant cards in a tarot reading reflect either the individual being read or the condition being enquired about. If the signature card is used to represent the individual, the majority of tarot readers prefer to use the courtroom card instead, either by comparing the inquirer's physical characteristics to one of the court cards or by associating their petroleum sign with one of the courtroom cards. If you choose a card to represent a specific situation, you can be as creative as you like. You may choose a card from the major or minor arcana, depending on the severity of the situation. The key arcana cards are used to address life's fundamental issues, whereas the minor arcana cards are used to address everyday concerns.

The critical card always directs your attention to the user profile you're reading about. Numerous tarot spreads feature prominently the significant cards. It enables the tarot reader to view the cards and identify the questioner's primary concerns.

3. Selecting the Appropriate Tarot Spread

Tarot Spreads are card patterns that follow a specific pattern. Within a set, each card location has a distinct meaning. After placing individual tarot cards in a tarot set, their meanings can be used to shape a plot. Following that, the tarot reader interprets the cards based on their location and relationships.

As a tarot reader, it is critical to choose a spread that correlates with the query. To begin, if the subject is love, you may wish to use a spread of love. In some instances, you may wish to create your own tarot spread. This is especially useful if the subject involves multiple issues.

4. Framing the Issue

How an inquirer constructs or asks a question prior to reading can have a significant impact on the overall utility of reading. The more personal the questioner is, the more likely the tarot reading will be able to resolve his dilemma in a specific way. Additionally, it is beneficial to keep the subject approachable. Open questions can reveal hidden or overlooked issues that might have gone unnoticed otherwise. Additionally, open-ended questions can assist the tarot reader in identifying critical issues or other factors that may affect the user.

5. Card Shuffle

There are numerous methods for matching cards when reading tarot. This is typically how the reader interacts with the cards (although some tarot readers do not allow anyone to handle their money). When you wish to delegate money management to the inquirer, you will ensure that the issues at hand are addressed while the cards are being shuffled, allowing the inquirer's focus to shift to the cards. There are several methods for "cutting" cards; the most common is for the inquirer to slice the deck three times with his left hand.

6. Becoming Familiar with Your Tarot Deck

Until I read some tarot, I continue to encourage people to take the time to truly appreciate the tarot deck they are working with.

This not only familiarises you with the games, but also helps you understand their definitions and how they communicate with one another. Naturally, those who receive a tarot reading from you will pick up on your relationship with your own cards. If you are unfamiliar with the deck with which you are working, this will almost certainly occur during a tarot reading.

Perfect Practice

Daily Exercise

To improve at a skill, particularly divination and Tarot reading, the most logical first step is to practise daily or as close to daily as possible. You're likely to begin with personal readings, as it's easier to discern how cards relate to you than it is to others.

After you've gained some familiarity with the cards, the next step would be to conduct readings for others. It is best to begin with close friends and family before branching out to strangers and eventually offering readings to near complete strangers. Ensure that you are completely comfortable with the readings at each stage of this step before proceeding to the next. Begin with small steps. If you dive into the deep end without first learning to swim, it is highly unlikely that you will survive.

New Interpretations

You may feel compelled to reinterpret a card during a reading, or even between readings, based on what the Divine places in your heart and mind.

This is not to say that you should disregard the card drawn and invent your own meaning every time. The card was chosen for a specific reason. The reason may not be the pre-determined meaning, but it will involve the card.

103

Formation of Habits

While some of this involves daily practise, the majority of it involves creating a divination ritual. Perhaps you have a particular area where card reading is made easier.

Incorporating the Cards into Your Life Take the following actions: Utilize the Cards Frequently

This is how you acquire the ability to read them in the first place.

Without frequent use, even on mundane tasks, proficiency, let alone mastery, will take an inordinate amount of time to achieve.

Avoid the following: Reliance Too Much on The Cards

They are not intended to be taken as absolutes. By taking the cards literally or anticipating events to unfold exactly as they are written, you set yourself up for failure and disappointment. Certain aspects of the cards may never come to pass. This is because you are aware of the outcome of your current path and work to make it as desirable as possible.

To Do: Experiment with a Variety of Spreads

When conducting readings, you want to select the spread that you believe will most completely address the question. There is no such thing as a one-size-fits-all spread that will cover all eventualities. As such, you should practise a variety of spreads in order to broaden your repertoire. Even if you believe you are familiar with a sufficient number of spreads, you may discover a new favourite that is more useful than any of the spreads.

Avoid the following: Become Disappointed

Do not be concerned if your readings are not 100 percent accurate. Few are in fact. Maintain your practise of readings and interpretations. They will improve over time and with effort. After a few failures, many beginners abandon their attempts. By failing, you only gain knowledge about how to succeed in the future. In most areas of life, practise makes perfect, and divination is no exception.

Maintain a Journal or a Notebook

This journal may be used for any purpose connected with Tarot. You can keep track of your accuracy by recording readings and interpretations along with the date and question. You may annotate cards with personal meanings. This is especially advantageous if you've redefined the majority, if not the entirety, of your deck. Additionally, you can keep track of your favourite spreads, taking note of the patterns and meanings associated with each card.

If you already own one, this journal may serve as your Book of Shadows or Grimoire.

Avoid Reliance on the Cards as a Fallback for Difficult Times

Hopefully, you won't encounter many significant problems in your life to apply the cards to. Having said that, if you only use the cards during times of turmoil, you won't get much practise, and you can't rely on your readings and interpretations to be as accurate as possible. Even mundane readings, such as a one-card response to the question "Should I get a burger or a salad?" help you hone your interpretation skills.

CONCLUSION

As you reach the end of this book, you would somehow realize that learning to read Tarot cards is more than fun and excitement. If you have mastered it the right way and applied it to change or enhance your present situation in life, you will realize that it is the best tool one should have. It may take time to memorize meanings but note that these tarot cards can connect to your inner mind.

The inner mind holds your spiritual knowledge and wisdom as well as your intuition and your inner critic. It's your inner consciousness that takes control of your life. By mastering how to use them to your advantage effectively, you can take control of your inner mind and use it to make better decisions to achieve your goals for a better and happier life.

www.ingramcontent.com/pod-product-compliance
Lightning Source LLC
LaVergne TN
LVHW041335200726
843509LV00009B/726